PERSONAL INFORMATION

Name:

Address:

Telephone: Email:

Employer:

Address:

Telephone: Email:

MEDICAL INFORMATION

Physician: Telephone:

Allergies:

Medications:

Blood Type:

Insurer:

IN CASE OF EMERGENCY, NOTIFY

Name:

Address:

Telephone: Relationship:

YOU are the reason we do what we do here at Barbour Publishing. We promise that we will always use our God-given talents to produce content with you in mind—and that we will remain biblically faithful, no matter what.

Thank you for being the heart of our business.

ISBN 979-8-89151-338-9

Published by Barbour Publishing, Inc., 1810 Barbour Drive, Uhrichsville, Ohio 44683, www.barbourbooks.com

Our mission is to inspire the world with the life-changing message of the Bible.

Printed in China.

2027
Creative Coloring
PLANNER

Introduction

It's easy to get bogged down in the responsibilities, to-do lists, and schedules of everyday life. But God gives us each day to quiet our hearts—to enter His presence and listen for His still, small voice.

Take time from your busy life to spend some one-on-one time with your heavenly Creator. This creative coloring planner is a good way to start. Use it to assist in the organization of the daily grind and allow the coloring pages and inspiring scriptures and prayers to bless your heart all 365 days of 2027.

2027

January

S	M	T	W	T	F	S
					1	2
3	4	5	6	7	8	9
10	11	12	13	14	15	16
17	18	19	20	21	22	23
24	25	26	27	28	29	30
31						

February

S	M	T	W	T	F	S
	1	2	3	4	5	6
7	8	9	10	11	12	13
14	15	16	17	18	19	20
21	22	23	24	25	26	27
28						

May

S	M	T	W	T	F	S
						1
2	3	4	5	6	7	8
9	10	11	12	13	14	15
16	17	18	19	20	21	22
23	24	25	26	27	28	29
30	31					

June

S	M	T	W	T	F	S
		1	2	3	4	5
6	7	8	9	10	11	12
13	14	15	16	17	18	19
20	21	22	23	24	25	26
27	28	29	30			

September

S	M	T	W	T	F	S
			1	2	3	4
5	6	7	8	9	10	11
12	13	14	15	16	17	18
19	20	21	22	23	24	25
26	27	28	29	30		

October

S	M	T	W	T	F	S
					1	2
3	4	5	6	7	8	9
10	11	12	13	14	15	16
17	18	19	20	21	22	23
24	25	26	27	28	29	30
31						

Year at a Glance

March

S	M	T	W	T	F	S
	1	2	3	4	5	6
7	8	9	10	11	12	13
14	15	16	17	18	19	20
21	22	23	24	25	26	27
28	29	30	31			

April

S	M	T	W	T	F	S
				1	2	3
4	5	6	7	8	9	10
11	12	13	14	15	16	17
18	19	20	21	22	23	24
25	26	27	28	29	30	

July

S	M	T	W	T	F	S
				1	2	3
4	5	6	7	8	9	10
11	12	13	14	15	16	17
18	19	20	21	22	23	24
25	26	27	28	29	30	31

August

S	M	T	W	T	F	S
1	2	3	4	5	6	7
8	9	10	11	12	13	14
15	16	17	18	19	20	21
22	23	24	25	26	27	28
29	30	31				

November

S	M	T	W	T	F	S
	1	2	3	4	5	6
7	8	9	10	11	12	13
14	15	16	17	18	19	20
21	22	23	24	25	26	27
28	29	30				

December

S	M	T	W	T	F	S
			1	2	3	4
5	6	7	8	9	10	11
12	13	14	15	16	17	18
19	20	21	22	23	24	25
26	27	28	29	30	31	

August 2026

SUNDAY	MONDAY	TUESDAY	WEDNESDAY
26	27	28	29
2	3	4	5
9	10	11	12
16	17	18	19
23 / 30	24 / 31	25	26

THURSDAY	FRIDAY	SATURDAY
30	31	1
6	7	8
13	14	15
20	21	22
27	28	29

notes

July

S	M	T	W	T	F	S
			1	2	3	4
5	6	7	8	9	10	11
12	13	14	15	16	17	18
19	20	21	22	23	24	25
26	27	28	29	30	31	

September

S	M	T	W	T	F	S
		1	2	3	4	5
6	7	8	9	10	11	12
13	14	15	16	17	18	19
20	21	22	23	24	25	26
27	28	29	30			

Heavenly Father,
MAY OUR
home
BE A PLACE OF
harmony.

Goals for the Month

Draw nigh to God,
and he will draw nigh to you.
James 4:8

July–August 2026

S	M	T	W	T	F	S
						1
2	3	4	5	6	7	8
9	10	11	12	13	14	15
16	17	18	19	20	21	22
23	24	25	26	27	28	29
30	31					

Every day there is something for which I can offer You praise, dear God! To begin with, we have the promise of a fresh start—a new opportunity to serve You. Throughout the day You show Your majesty in a multitude of ways. You are an awesome God!

to-do list

- [ ]
- [ ]
- [ ]
- [ ]
- [ ]
- [ ]
- [ ]
- [ ]
- [ ]
- [ ]
- [ ]
- [ ]
- [ ]
- [ ]
- [ ]

SUNDAY, July 26

MONDAY, July 27

TUESDAY, July 28

WEDNESDAY, July 29

THURSDAY, July 30

FRIDAY, July 31

SATURDAY, August 1

to-do list

- [ ]
- [ ]
- [ ]
- [ ]
- [ ]
- [ ]
- [ ]
- [ ]
- [ ]
- [ ]
- [ ]
- [ ]
- [ ]
- [ ]
- [ ]
- [ ]

But seek ye first the
kingdom of God,
and his righteousness;
and all these things shall
be added unto you.
MATTHEW 6:33

August 2026

S	M	T	W	T	F	S
						1
2	3	4	5	6	7	8
9	10	11	12	13	14	15
16	17	18	19	20	21	22
23	24	25	26	27	28	29
30	31					

Lord, I know that in the center of Your will are peace, joy, and many other rich blessings. I'd like to experience all these things. Please help me be attentive when You speak, and give me a heart willing to be used by You.

to-do list

- [ ] ....
- [ ] ....
- [ ] ....
- [ ] ....
- [ ] ....
- [ ] ....
- [ ] ....
- [ ] ....
- [ ] ....
- [ ] ....
- [ ] ....
- [ ] ....
- [ ] ....
- [ ] ....
- [ ] ....

SUNDAY, August 2

MONDAY, August 3

TUESDAY, August 4

WEDNESDAY, August 5

THURSDAY, August 6

FRIDAY, August 7

SATURDAY, August 8

to-do list

- [ ]
- [ ]
- [ ]
- [ ]
- [ ]
- [ ]
- [ ]
- [ ]
- [ ]
- [ ]
- [ ]
- [ ]
- [ ]
- [ ]
- [ ]
- [ ]

And he said, The God of our fathers hath chosen thee, that thou shouldest know his will, and see that Just One, and shouldest hear the voice of his mouth.

ACTS 22:14

August 2026

S	M	T	W	T	F	S
						1
2	3	4	5	6	7	8
9	10	11	12	13	14	15
16	17	18	19	20	21	22
23	24	25	26	27	28	29
30	31					

Your desire is that we seek and do Your will, dear God, but You'll never force us to do it. You've laid unique paths before each of us, and it's because You love us all in a special way. Help us not to envy Your plans for others; let us complete our work with joy.

to-do list

- [ ]
- [ ]
- [ ]
- [ ]
- [ ]
- [ ]
- [ ]
- [ ]
- [ ]
- [ ]
- [ ]
- [ ]
- [ ]
- [ ]
- [ ]

SUNDAY, August 9

MONDAY, August 10

TUESDAY, August 11

WEDNESDAY, August 12

THURSDAY, August 13

FRIDAY, August 14

SATURDAY, August 15

to-do list

And God is able to make all grace abound toward you; that ye, always having all sufficiency in all things, may abound to every good work.

2 Corinthians 9:8

August 2026

S	M	T	W	T	F	S
						1
2	3	4	5	6	7	8
9	10	11	12	13	14	15
16	17	18	19	20	21	22
23	24	25	26	27	28	29
30	31					

You wanted to use me, Father, but You knew there were areas in my heart that first needed cleansing. You knew the only way to accomplish this would be to send purifying flames. The testing fires were painful sometimes, but I'm glad You sent them. It felt good to be washed and worthy of service.

to-do list

- [ ]
- [ ]
- [ ]
- [ ]
- [ ]
- [ ]
- [ ]
- [ ]
- [ ]
- [ ]
- [ ]
- [ ]
- [ ]
- [ ]
- [ ]

SUNDAY, August 16

MONDAY, August 17

TUESDAY, August 18

WEDNESDAY, August 19

THURSDAY, August 20

FRIDAY, August 21

SATURDAY, August 22

to-do list

Not by works of righteousness which we have done, but according to his mercy he saved us, by the washing of regeneration, and renewing of the Holy Ghost.

TITUS 3:5

August 2026

S	M	T	W	T	F	S
						1
2	3	4	5	6	7	8
9	10	11	12	13	14	15
16	17	18	19	20	21	22
23	24	25	26	27	28	29
30	31					

Dear Jesus, I've known many people in my life. My relationship with You is the most important. I'm so glad You have time for me and that You want me to fellowship with You. I couldn't ask for a better friend.

to-do list

- [ ]
- [ ]
- [ ]
- [ ]
- [ ]
- [ ]
- [ ]
- [ ]
- [ ]
- [ ]
- [ ]
- [ ]
- [ ]
- [ ]
- [ ]

SUNDAY, August 23

MONDAY, August 24

TUESDAY, August 25

WEDNESDAY, August 26

THURSDAY, August 27

FRIDAY, August 28

SATURDAY, August 29

to-do list

Jesus answered and said unto him, If a man love me, he will keep my words: and my Father will love him, and we will come unto him, and make our abode with him.

JOHN 14:23

September 2026

SUNDAY	MONDAY	TUESDAY	WEDNESDAY
30	31	1	2
6	7 *Labor Day*	8	9
13	14	15	16
20	21	22 *First Day of Autumn*	23 *See You at the Pole*
27	28	29	30

THURSDAY	FRIDAY	SATURDAY
3	4	5
10	11	12
17	18	19
24	25	26
1	2	3

notes

August

S	M	T	W	T	F	S
						1
2	3	4	5	6	7	8
9	10	11	12	13	14	15
16	17	18	19	20	21	22
23	24	25	26	27	28	29
30	31					

October

S	M	T	W	T	F	S
				1	2	3
4	5	6	7	8	9	10
11	12	13	14	15	16	17
18	19	20	21	22	23	24
25	26	27	28	29	30	31

Lord, draw me always closer to You.

Goals for the Month

These things I have spoken unto you, that in me ye might have peace. In the world ye shall have tribulation: but be of good cheer; I have overcome the world.

JOHN 16:33

August–September 2026

S	M	T	W	T	F	S
		1	2	3	4	5
6	7	8	9	10	11	12
13	14	15	16	17	18	19
20	21	22	23	24	25	26
27	28	29	30			

I find it difficult to even sit down to a meal, Father. Resting seems like such a far-fetched notion. I know You want me to find time to rest and spend time with You, but I'm on the go constantly, and I still don't get everything done. Please help me, Lord, to make resting a priority.

to-do list

- [ ]
- [ ]
- [ ]
- [ ]
- [ ]
- [ ]
- [ ]
- [ ]
- [ ]
- [ ]
- [ ]
- [ ]
- [ ]
- [ ]
- [ ]

SUNDAY, August 30

MONDAY, August 31

TUESDAY, September 1

WEDNESDAY, September 2

THURSDAY, September 3

FRIDAY, September 4

SATURDAY, September 5

to-do list

Take my yoke upon you, and learn of me; for I am meek and lowly in heart: and ye shall find rest unto your souls.

MATTHEW 11:29

September 2026

S	M	T	W	T	F	S
		1	2	3	4	5
6	7	8	9	10	11	12
13	14	15	16	17	18	19
20	21	22	23	24	25	26
27	28	29	30			

Salvation is something we all long for in one way or another, Father, and the salvation You've provided far surpasses anything that could be presented by mankind. You've rescued me from the depths of sin and given me new life in Christ, and I will ever praise You!

to-do list

- [ ]
- [ ]
- [ ]
- [ ]
- [ ]
- [ ]
- [ ]
- [ ]
- [ ]
- [ ]
- [ ]
- [ ]
- [ ]
- [ ]
- [ ]

SUNDAY, September 6

MONDAY, September 7 *Labor Day*

TUESDAY, September 8

WEDNESDAY, September 9

THURSDAY, September 10

FRIDAY, September 11

SATURDAY, September 12

to-do list

For by grace are ye saved through faith; and that not of yourselves: it is the gift of God.
EPHESIANS 2:8

September 2026

S	M	T	W	T	F	S
		1	2	3	4	5
6	7	8	9	10	11	12
13	14	15	16	17	18	19
20	21	22	23	24	25	26
27	28	29	30			

You said that accepting You requires childlike faith, dear Jesus. Yet so often we fail to take the young ones seriously. We think they're too young to understand, but You said to let them come. Give us wisdom when dealing with the little ones, and help us encourage them to accept You as well.

to-do list

- [ ]
- [ ]
- [ ]
- [ ]
- [ ]
- [ ]
- [ ]
- [ ]
- [ ]
- [ ]
- [ ]
- [ ]
- [ ]
- [ ]
- [ ]

SUNDAY, September 13

MONDAY, September 14

TUESDAY, September 15

WEDNESDAY, September 16

THURSDAY, September 17

FRIDAY, September 18

SATURDAY, September 19

to-do list

- [ ]
- [ ]
- [ ]
- [ ]
- [ ]
- [ ]
- [ ]
- [ ]
- [ ]
- [ ]
- [ ]
- [ ]
- [ ]
- [ ]
- [ ]
- [ ]

Verily I say unto you, Whosoever shall not receive the kingdom of God as a little child, he shall not enter therein.

MARK 10:15

September 2026

S	M	T	W	T	F	S
		1	2	3	4	5
6	7	8	9	10	11	12
13	14	15	16	17	18	19
20	21	22	23	24	25	26
27	28	29	30			

We are such a frenetic lot, dear God, but when we get all worked up, You say, "Stand still." You offer complete salvation but only when we take the time to see from where our deliverance comes. Help us slow down and witness the greatest of miracles.

to-do list

- [ ]
- [ ]
- [ ]
- [ ]
- [ ]
- [ ]
- [ ]
- [ ]
- [ ]
- [ ]
- [ ]
- [ ]
- [ ]
- [ ]
- [ ]

SUNDAY, September 20

MONDAY, September 21

TUESDAY, September 22 *First Day of Autumn*

WEDNESDAY, September 23 *See You at the Pole*

THURSDAY, September 24

FRIDAY, September 25

SATURDAY, September 26

to-do list

And we know that the Son of God is come, and hath given us an understanding, that we may know him that is true, and we are in him that is true, even in his Son Jesus Christ. This is the true God, and eternal life.

1 John 5:20

September–October 2026

S	M	T	W	T	F	S
		1	2	3	4	5
6	7	8	9	10	11	12
13	14	15	16	17	18	19
20	21	22	23	24	25	26
27	28	29	30			

Father, You created me in Your image. For that I am thankful, but I need to remember that I'm not perfect. Help me not to be proud but to daily strive to be more like You.

to-do list

- [ ]
- [ ]
- [ ]
- [ ]
- [ ]
- [ ]
- [ ]
- [ ]
- [ ]
- [ ]
- [ ]
- [ ]
- [ ]
- [ ]
- [ ]

SUNDAY, September 27

MONDAY, September 28

TUESDAY, September 29

WEDNESDAY, September 30

THURSDAY, October 1

FRIDAY, October 2

SATURDAY, October 3

to-do list

- [ ]
- [ ]
- [ ]
- [ ]
- [ ]
- [ ]
- [ ]
- [ ]
- [ ]
- [ ]
- [ ]
- [ ]
- [ ]
- [ ]
- [ ]
- [ ]

Be of the same mind one toward another. Mind not high things, but condescend to men of low estate. Be not wise in your own conceits.

ROMANS 12:16

October 2026

SUNDAY	MONDAY	TUESDAY	WEDNESDAY
27	28	29	30
4	5	6	7
11	12 *Columbus Day*	13	14
18	19	20	21
25	26	27	28

THURSDAY	FRIDAY	SATURDAY
1	2	3
8	9	10
15	16	17
22	23	24
29	30	31 *Halloween*

notes

September

S	M	T	W	T	F	S
		1	2	3	4	5
6	7	8	9	10	11	12
13	14	15	16	17	18	19
20	21	22	23	24	25	26
27	28	29	30			

November

S	M	T	W	T	F	S
1	2	3	4	5	6	7
8	9	10	11	12	13	14
15	16	17	18	19	20	21
22	23	24	25	26	27	28
29	30					

Father God,
thank You for the work
of Your hands.

Goals for the Month

The humble will see their God at work and be glad. Let all who seek God's help be encouraged.
PSALM 69:32 NLT

October 2026

S	M	T	W	T	F	S
				1	2	3
4	5	6	7	8	9	10
11	12	13	14	15	16	17
18	19	20	21	22	23	24
25	26	27	28	29	30	31

You've promised to walk with me all the way and provide all that I need, dear God, and I'm rejoicing in that guarantee. What more do I need? It doesn't matter that the world presents shiny trinkets. Their luster dims in the brilliance of the blessings and contentment that You give.

to-do list

- [ ]
- [ ]
- [ ]
- [ ]
- [ ]
- [ ]
- [ ]
- [ ]
- [ ]
- [ ]
- [ ]
- [ ]
- [ ]
- [ ]
- [ ]

SUNDAY, October 4

MONDAY, October 5

TUESDAY, October 6

WEDNESDAY, October 7

THURSDAY, October 8

FRIDAY, October 9

SATURDAY, October 10

to-do list

- [ ]
- [ ]
- [ ]
- [ ]
- [ ]
- [ ]
- [ ]
- [ ]
- [ ]
- [ ]
- [ ]
- [ ]
- [ ]
- [ ]
- [ ]
- [ ]

Let your conversation be without covetousness; and be content with such things as ye have: for he hath said, I will never leave thee, nor forsake thee.

HEBREWS 13:5

October 2026

S	M	T	W	T	F	S
				1	2	3
4	5	6	7	8	9	10
11	12	13	14	15	16	17
18	19	20	21	22	23	24
25	26	27	28	29	30	31

You gave me an amazing opportunity today, Father, and it's all a result of a discouraging situation. You helped me as I struggled through the problem, and because of that I was able to encourage someone else who faced a similar difficulty. You really are an awesome God!

to-do list

- [ ]
- [ ]
- [ ]
- [ ]
- [ ]
- [ ]
- [ ]
- [ ]
- [ ]
- [ ]
- [ ]
- [ ]
- [ ]
- [ ]
- [ ]

SUNDAY, October 11

MONDAY, October 12 *Columbus Day*

TUESDAY, October 13

WEDNESDAY, October 14

THURSDAY, October 15

FRIDAY, October 16

SATURDAY, October 17

to-do list

- [ ]
- [ ]
- [ ]
- [ ]
- [ ]
- [ ]
- [ ]
- [ ]
- [ ]
- [ ]
- [ ]
- [ ]
- [ ]
- [ ]
- [ ]
- [ ]

Anxious hearts are very heavy, but a word of encouragement does wonders!

PROVERBS 12:25 TLB

October 2026

S	M	T	W	T	F	S
				1	2	3
4	5	6	7	8	9	10
11	12	13	14	15	16	17
18	19	20	21	22	23	24
25	26	27	28	29	30	31

It's so hard to express grief in our society, Jesus, but I'm glad You don't reject us when we do. After all, You grieved, and You showed me how to handle perhaps one of the deepest human emotions. Thank You for letting me come to You when I'm hurting. Thank You for Your love.

to-do list

- [ ]
- [ ]
- [ ]
- [ ]
- [ ]
- [ ]
- [ ]
- [ ]
- [ ]
- [ ]
- [ ]
- [ ]
- [ ]
- [ ]
- [ ]

SUNDAY, October 18

MONDAY, October 19

TUESDAY, October 20

WEDNESDAY, October 21

THURSDAY, October 22

FRIDAY, October 23

SATURDAY, October 24

to-do list

But the God of all grace, who hath called us unto his eternal glory by Christ Jesus, after that ye have suffered a while, make you perfect, stablish, strengthen, settle you.

1 PETER 5:10

October 2026

S	M	T	W	T	F	S
				1	2	3
4	5	6	7	8	9	10
11	12	13	14	15	16	17
18	19	20	21	22	23	24
25	26	27	28	29	30	31

How can I doubt my worth in Your eyes, Father? You know the number of hairs on my head. You created me, and You said that Your creation is very good. When I'm tempted to get down on myself, remind me that I am special to You and that there's no one just like me.

to-do list

- [ ]
- [ ]
- [ ]
- [ ]
- [ ]
- [ ]
- [ ]
- [ ]
- [ ]
- [ ]
- [ ]
- [ ]
- [ ]
- [ ]
- [ ]

SUNDAY, October 25

MONDAY, October 26

TUESDAY, October 27

WEDNESDAY, October 28

THURSDAY, October 29

FRIDAY, October 30

SATURDAY, October 31 *Halloween*

to-do list

- [ ]
- [ ]
- [ ]
- [ ]
- [ ]
- [ ]
- [ ]
- [ ]
- [ ]
- [ ]
- [ ]
- [ ]
- [ ]
- [ ]
- [ ]
- [ ]

You made all the delicate, inner parts of my body and knit me together in my mother's womb.
PSALM 139:13 NLT

November 2026

SUNDAY	MONDAY	TUESDAY	WEDNESDAY
1 *Daylight Saving Time Ends*	2	3 *Election Day*	4
8	9	10	11 *Veterans Day*
15	16	17	18
22	23	24	25
29	30	1	2

THURSDAY	FRIDAY	SATURDAY
5	6	7
12	13	14
19	20	21
26 *Thanksgiving Day*	27	28
3	4	5

notes

October

S	M	T	W	T	F	S
				1	2	3
4	5	6	7	8	9	10
11	12	13	14	15	16	17
18	19	20	21	22	23	24
25	26	27	28	29	30	31

December

S	M	T	W	T	F	S
		1	2	3	4	5
6	7	8	9	10	11	12
13	14	15	16	17	18	19
20	21	22	23	24	25	26
27	28	29	30	31		

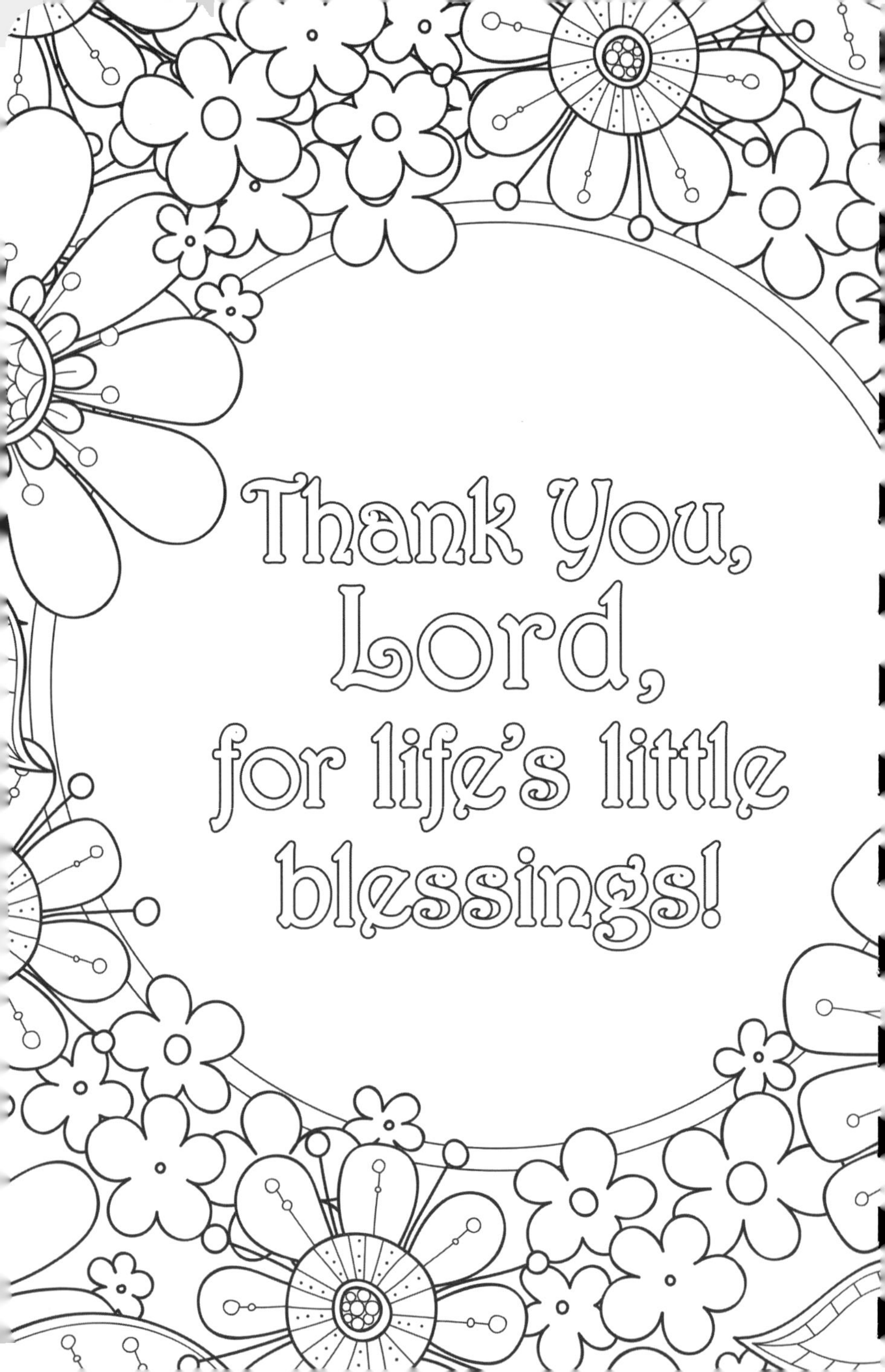
Thank You,
Lord,
for life's little
blessings!

Goals for the Month

My power and my strength
come from the Lord,
and he has saved me.
Psalm 118:14 CEV

November 2026

S	M	T	W	T	F	S
1	2	3	4	5	6	7
8	9	10	11	12	13	14
15	16	17	18	19	20	21
22	23	24	25	26	27	28
29	30					

Thank You for the many happy times You've given me. So often it's the little things in life—the first robin in the spring, the first homegrown tomato of the season, even a brilliant sunset. These simple blessings evoke the biggest smiles and make me the happiest!

to-do list

- [ ]
- [ ]
- [ ]
- [ ]
- [ ]
- [ ]
- [ ]
- [ ]
- [ ]
- [ ]
- [ ]
- [ ]
- [ ]
- [ ]
- [ ]

SUNDAY, November 1 *Daylight Saving Time Ends*

MONDAY, November 2

TUESDAY, November 3 *Election Day*

WEDNESDAY, November 4

THURSDAY, November 5

FRIDAY, November 6

SATURDAY, November 7

to-do list

It is of the L*ORD's mercies that we are not consumed, because his compassions fail not. They are new every morning: great is thy faithfulness.*

LAMENTATIONS 3:22–23

November 2026

S	M	T	W	T	F	S
1	2	3	4	5	6	7
8	9	10	11	12	13	14
15	16	17	18	19	20	21
22	23	24	25	26	27	28
29	30					

Stress seems so overrated these days, doesn't it, Lord? Every time I turn around, someone is telling me how stressed they are. And I do the same thing. I guess it's popular to be stressed. Popular maybe—but not good. Please take my stress and turn it into energy that is used for Your glory.

to-do list

- [ ]
- [ ]
- [ ]
- [ ]
- [ ]
- [ ]
- [ ]
- [ ]
- [ ]
- [ ]
- [ ]
- [ ]
- [ ]
- [ ]
- [ ]

SUNDAY, November 8

MONDAY, November 9

TUESDAY, November 10

WEDNESDAY, November 11 *Veterans Day*

THURSDAY, November 12

FRIDAY, November 13

SATURDAY, November 14

to-do list

- [ ]
- [ ]
- [ ]
- [ ]
- [ ]
- [ ]
- [ ]
- [ ]
- [ ]
- [ ]
- [ ]
- [ ]
- [ ]
- [ ]
- [ ]
- [ ]

But you are a chosen generation, a royal priesthood, a holy nation, His own special people, that you may proclaim the praises of Him who called you out of darkness into His marvelous light.

1 PETER 2:9 NKJV

November 2026

S	M	T	W	T	F	S
1	2	3	4	5	6	7
8	9	10	11	12	13	14
15	16	17	18	19	20	21
22	23	24	25	26	27	28
29	30					

I'm glad money isn't required to obtain true happiness, or I wouldn't get much. You meet my needs sufficiently, but the happiness I enjoy when I'm with family or just relaxing with a good book on a lazy afternoon is beyond sufficient. True happiness really can't be bought, can it, Jesus?

to-do list

- [ ]
- [ ]
- [ ]
- [ ]
- [ ]
- [ ]
- [ ]
- [ ]
- [ ]
- [ ]
- [ ]
- [ ]
- [ ]
- [ ]
- [ ]

SUNDAY, November 15

MONDAY, November 16

TUESDAY, November 17

WEDNESDAY, November 18

THURSDAY, November 19

FRIDAY, November 20

SATURDAY, November 21

to-do list

Happy is that people,
that is in such a case:
yea, happy is that people,
whose God is the LORD.
PSALM 144:15

November 2026

S	M	T	W	T	F	S
1	2	3	4	5	6	7
8	9	10	11	12	13	14
15	16	17	18	19	20	21
22	23	24	25	26	27	28
29	30					

Sometimes I get pretty confused, Lord. I try to eat right, exercise properly, and get plenty of rest, but all the "experts" say different things about what I should be doing. It's important that I am a good steward of the body You've given me, so please help me to care for myself the right way.

to-do list

- [ ]
- [ ]
- [ ]
- [ ]
- [ ]
- [ ]
- [ ]
- [ ]
- [ ]
- [ ]
- [ ]
- [ ]
- [ ]
- [ ]
- [ ]

SUNDAY, November 22

MONDAY, November 23

TUESDAY, November 24

WEDNESDAY, November 25

THURSDAY, November 26 *Thanksgiving Day*

FRIDAY, November 27

SATURDAY, November 28

to-do list

- [ ]
- [ ]
- [ ]
- [ ]
- [ ]
- [ ]
- [ ]
- [ ]
- [ ]
- [ ]
- [ ]
- [ ]
- [ ]
- [ ]
- [ ]
- [ ]

Do you not know that your bodies are temples of the Holy Spirit, who is in you, whom you have received from God? You are not your own; you were bought at a price. Therefore honor God with your bodies.

1 Corinthians 6:19–20 niv

December 2026

SUNDAY	MONDAY	TUESDAY	WEDNESDAY
29	30	1	2
6	7	8	9
13	14	15	16
20	21 *First Day of Winter*	22	23
27	28	29	30

THURSDAY	FRIDAY	SATURDAY
3	4 *Hanukkah Begins at Sundown*	5
10	11	12
17	18	19
24 *Christmas Eve*	25 *Christmas Day*	26
31 *New Year's Eve*	1	2

notes

November

S	M	T	W	T	F	S
1	2	3	4	5	6	7
8	9	10	11	12	13	14
15	16	17	18	19	20	21
22	23	24	25	26	27	28
29	30					

January

S	M	T	W	T	F	S
					1	2
3	4	5	6	7	8	9
10	11	12	13	14	15	16
17	18	19	20	21	22	23
24	25	26	27	28	29	30
31						

Father God,
Your calm presence
restores my soul.

Goals for the Month

I can always count on you—
God, my dependable love.
Psalm 59:17 msg

November–December 2026

S	M	T	W	T	F	S
		1	2	3	4	5
6	7	8	9	10	11	12
13	14	15	16	17	18	19
20	21	22	23	24	25	26
27	28	29	30	31		

I'm so forgetful! God, I know how many times You've admonished me to seek Your wisdom, yet over and over I try to do things on my own. You'd think I would learn after so many mistakes, but I guess I'm too proud. I don't want to continue like this. I want Your wisdom so that I can live life as You intended.

to-do list

- [ ]
- [ ]
- [ ]
- [ ]
- [ ]
- [ ]
- [ ]
- [ ]
- [ ]
- [ ]
- [ ]
- [ ]
- [ ]
- [ ]
- [ ]

SUNDAY, November 29

MONDAY, November 30

TUESDAY, December 1

WEDNESDAY, December 2

THURSDAY, December 3

FRIDAY, December 4

Hanukkah Begins at Sundown

SATURDAY, December 5

to-do list

For the Lord gives wisdom; from His mouth come knowledge and understanding.
PROVERBS 2:6 NKJV

December 2026

S	M	T	W	T	F	S
		1	2	3	4	5
6	7	8	9	10	11	12
13	14	15	16	17	18	19
20	21	22	23	24	25	26
27	28	29	30	31		

There are many ways to be involved in my community, Father, and I ask You to show me what to do. I want to choose the activities that will help others and that will bring glory to You. Help me to weigh the possibilities carefully and to make the best decisions. Thank You for these opportunities to honor You.

to-do list

- [ ]
- [ ]
- [ ]
- [ ]
- [ ]
- [ ]
- [ ]
- [ ]
- [ ]
- [ ]
- [ ]
- [ ]
- [ ]
- [ ]
- [ ]

SUNDAY, December 6

MONDAY, December 7

TUESDAY, December 8

WEDNESDAY, December 9

THURSDAY, December 10

FRIDAY, December 11

SATURDAY, December 12

to-do list

Give unto the LORD *the glory due to His name; worship the* LORD *in the beauty of holiness.*

PSALM 29:2 NKJV

December 2026

S	M	T	W	T	F	S
		1	2	3	4	5
6	7	8	9	10	11	12
13	14	15	16	17	18	19
20	21	22	23	24	25	26
27	28	29	30	31		

You brought healing to so many people in the Bible, Jesus. Those were exciting times for those individuals, and it's still a spectacular miracle when You make someone whole today. Thank You for the many times You've touched my sick body or brought relief to my loved ones. Your loving touch produces great joy.

to-do list

- [ ]
- [ ]
- [ ]
- [ ]
- [ ]
- [ ]
- [ ]
- [ ]
- [ ]
- [ ]
- [ ]
- [ ]
- [ ]
- [ ]
- [ ]

SUNDAY, December 13

MONDAY, December 14

TUESDAY, December 15

WEDNESDAY, December 16

THURSDAY, December 17

FRIDAY, December 18

SATURDAY, December 19

to-do list

Is anyone among you suffering? . . . Is anyone among you sick? . . . And the prayer of faith will save the sick, and the Lord will raise him up.

JAMES 5:13–15 NKJV

December 2026

S	M	T	W	T	F	S
		1	2	3	4	5
6	7	8	9	10	11	12
13	14	15	16	17	18	19
20	21	22	23	24	25	26
27	28	29	30	31		

I've heard it said that home is where the heart is, and I suppose there's a lot of truth in that. My home is such a special place, and it seems that often when I'm somewhere else, I am longing to be back in that place, surrounded by what is comfortable and familiar. Thank You, Father, for that opportunity to return home.

to-do list

SUNDAY, December 20

MONDAY, December 21 *First Day of Winter*

TUESDAY, December 22

WEDNESDAY, December 23

THURSDAY, December 24 *Christmas Eve*

FRIDAY, December 25 *Christmas Day*

SATURDAY, December 26

to-do list

And I will give them an heart to know me, that I am the Lord: and they shall be my people, and I will be their God: for they shall return unto me with their whole heart.

Jeremiah 24:7

January 2027

SUNDAY	MONDAY	TUESDAY	WEDNESDAY
27	28	29	30
3	4	5	6
10	11	12	13
17	18 *Martin Luther King Jr. Day*	19	20
24 / 31	25	26	27

THURSDAY	FRIDAY	SATURDAY
31	1 *New Year's Day*	2
7	8	9
14	15	16
21	22	23
28	29	30

notes

December

S	M	T	W	T	F	S
		1	2	3	4	5
6	7	8	9	10	11	12
13	14	15	16	17	18	19
20	21	22	23	24	25	26
27	28	29	30	31		

February

S	M	T	W	T	F	S
	1	2	3	4	5	6
7	8	9	10	11	12	13
14	15	16	17	18	19	20
21	22	23	24	25	26	27
28						

Goals for the Month

Pile your troubles on God's shoulders—he'll carry your load, he'll help you out.
Psalm 55:22 MSG

December 2026–January 2027

S	M	T	W	T	F	S
					1	2
3	4	5	6	7	8	9
10	11	12	13	14	15	16
17	18	19	20	21	22	23
24	25	26	27	28	29	30
31						

Dear God, I'm a far cry from perfect, but I'm confident in the knowledge that You love me just as I am. You are the one who has begun a work in me, and You will be faithful to complete what has been started. What a thrill to know that You'll make me what You want me to be.

to-do list

- [ ] ....
- [ ] ....
- [ ] ....
- [ ] ....
- [ ] ....
- [ ] ....
- [ ] ....
- [ ] ....
- [ ] ....
- [ ] ....
- [ ] ....
- [ ] ....
- [ ] ....
- [ ] ....
- [ ] ....

SUNDAY, December 27

MONDAY, December 28

TUESDAY, December 29

WEDNESDAY, December 30

THURSDAY, December 31 *New Year's Eve*

FRIDAY, January 1 *New Year's Day*

SATURDAY, January 2

to-do list

"Therefore know that the LORD your God, He is God, the faithful God who keeps covenant and mercy for a thousand generations with those who love Him and keep His commandments."

DEUTERONOMY 7:9 NKJV

January 2027

S	M	T	W	T	F	S
					1	2
3	4	5	6	7	8	9
10	11	12	13	14	15	16
17	18	19	20	21	22	23
24	25	26	27	28	29	30
31						

I can't take it, Father. It sometimes seems like others deliberately do things to upset me. Maybe it's just how they are with everyone, but I have trouble not retaliating. I try so hard to be like You, but it's a struggle. Please help me control my anger; help me not to be so sensitive.

to-do list

- [ ]
- [ ]
- [ ]
- [ ]
- [ ]
- [ ]
- [ ]
- [ ]
- [ ]
- [ ]
- [ ]
- [ ]
- [ ]
- [ ]
- [ ]

SUNDAY, January 3

MONDAY, January 4

TUESDAY, January 5

WEDNESDAY, January 6

THURSDAY, January 7

FRIDAY, January 8

SATURDAY, January 9

to-do list

Don't have anything to do with foolish and stupid arguments, because you know they produce quarrels. And the Lord's servant must not be quarrelsome but must be kind to everyone, able to teach, not resentful.

2 TIMOTHY 2:23–24 NIV

January 2027

S	M	T	W	T	F	S
					1	2
3	4	5	6	7	8	9
10	11	12	13	14	15	16
17	18	19	20	21	22	23
24	25	26	27	28	29	30
31						

I did it again, Lord. I ruined an entire evening because of something incredibly ridiculous. I didn't sleep well because I was still fuming. My anger is always such a waste of time and energy. Forgive me, Father. Give me strength to control my temper, and don't let me ruin any more evenings for myself or for others.

to-do list

- [ ]
- [ ]
- [ ]
- [ ]
- [ ]
- [ ]
- [ ]
- [ ]
- [ ]
- [ ]
- [ ]
- [ ]
- [ ]
- [ ]
- [ ]

SUNDAY, January 10

MONDAY, January 11

TUESDAY, January 12

WEDNESDAY, January 13

THURSDAY, January 14

FRIDAY, January 15

SATURDAY, January 16

to-do list

Wherefore, my beloved brethren, let every man be swift to hear, slow to speak, slow to wrath: for the wrath of man worketh not the righteousness of God.

James 1:19–20

January 2027

S	M	T	W	T	F	S
					1	2
3	4	5	6	7	8	9
10	11	12	13	14	15	16
17	18	19	20	21	22	23
24	25	26	27	28	29	30
31						

to-do list

- [ ]
- [ ]
- [ ]
- [ ]
- [ ]
- [ ]
- [ ]
- [ ]
- [ ]
- [ ]
- [ ]
- [ ]
- [ ]
- [ ]
- [ ]

Since You came into my life, dear Jesus, I am filled with a fascinating joy. You've given me a new song, and I find myself singing it at the most unusual times. Sometimes I receive questioning looks, but it gives me an opportunity to share with others what You've done in my life. I pray they seek Your joy too.

SUNDAY, January 17

MONDAY, January 18 *Martin Luther King Jr. Day*

TUESDAY, January 19

WEDNESDAY, January 20

THURSDAY, January 21

FRIDAY, January 22

SATURDAY, January 23

to-do list

Let the word of Christ dwell in you richly in all wisdom; teaching and admonishing one another in psalms and hymns and spiritual songs, singing with grace in your hearts to the Lord.

Colossians 3:16

January 2027

S	M	T	W	T	F	S
					1	2
3	4	5	6	7	8	9
10	11	12	13	14	15	16
17	18	19	20	21	22	23
24	25	26	27	28	29	30
31						

Thank You for my pastor, dear God. He loves You; and he loves those to whom he ministers. Knowing that his desire is to present the truths of the Bible is a great comfort in a world that is full of false teachings. Bless my pastor as he continues to preach Your Word.

to-do list

- [ ]
- [ ]
- [ ]
- [ ]
- [ ]
- [ ]
- [ ]
- [ ]
- [ ]
- [ ]
- [ ]
- [ ]
- [ ]
- [ ]
- [ ]

SUNDAY, January 24

MONDAY, January 25

TUESDAY, January 26

WEDNESDAY, January 27

THURSDAY, January 28

FRIDAY, January 29

SATURDAY, January 30

to-do list

Let the elders that rule well be counted worthy of double honour, especially they who labour in the word and doctrine.

1 Timothy 5:17

February 2027

SUNDAY	MONDAY	TUESDAY	WEDNESDAY
31	1	2	3
7	8	9	10 *Ash Wednesday*
14 *Valentine's Day*	15 *Presidents' Day*	16	17
21	22	23	24
28	1	2	3

THURSDAY	FRIDAY	SATURDAY
4	5	6
11	12	13
18	19	20
25	26	27
4	5	6

notes

January

S	M	T	W	T	F	S
					1	2
3	4	5	6	7	8	9
10	11	12	13	14	15	16
17	18	19	20	21	22	23
24	25	26	27	28	29	30
31						

March

S	M	T	W	T	F	S
	1	2	3	4	5	6
7	8	9	10	11	12	13
14	15	16	17	18	19	20
21	22	23	24	25	26	27
28	29	30	31			

Lord, give me a heart of joy.

Goals for the Month

And may the Lord our God
show us his approval and make
our efforts successful. Yes,
make our efforts successful!
PSALM 90:17 NLT

January–February 2027

S	M	T	W	T	F	S
	1	2	3	4	5	6
7	8	9	10	11	12	13
14	15	16	17	18	19	20
21	22	23	24	25	26	27
28						

Although the world might not think that my circumstances always warrant a song, I am rejoicing in the knowledge of what lies ahead. I have perfect hope of an eternity with You. I have joy in the belief that You are with me each step of the way. You have put a smile in my heart. Thank You, Lord.

to-do list

- [ ]
- [ ]
- [ ]
- [ ]
- [ ]
- [ ]
- [ ]
- [ ]
- [ ]
- [ ]
- [ ]
- [ ]
- [ ]
- [ ]
- [ ]

SUNDAY, January 31

MONDAY, February 1

TUESDAY, February 2

WEDNESDAY, February 3

THURSDAY, February 4

FRIDAY, February 5

SATURDAY, February 6

to-do list

Surely goodness and mercy shall follow me all the days of my life: and I will dwell in the house of the LORD *for ever.*

PSALM 23:6

February 2027

S	M	T	W	T	F	S
	1	2	3	4	5	6
7	8	9	10	11	12	13
14	15	16	17	18	19	20
21	22	23	24	25	26	27
28						

Sometimes I get a little discouraged, Jesus. I feel like I've reached all the goals I've set for myself and that there's nothing for me to achieve that would bring any excitement. Please give me a new outlook. Give me wisdom as I set new goals, and help me to give You the glory when I succeed.

to-do list

- [ ]
- [ ]
- [ ]
- [ ]
- [ ]
- [ ]
- [ ]
- [ ]
- [ ]
- [ ]
- [ ]
- [ ]
- [ ]
- [ ]
- [ ]

SUNDAY, February 7

MONDAY, February 8

TUESDAY, February 9

WEDNESDAY, February 10 *Ash Wednesday*

THURSDAY, February 11

FRIDAY, February 12

SATURDAY, February 13

to-do list

Listen to advice and accept discipline, so that you may be wise the rest of your days.
PROVERBS 19:20 NASB

February 2027

S	M	T	W	T	F	S
	1	2	3	4	5	6
7	8	9	10	11	12	13
14	15	16	17	18	19	20
21	22	23	24	25	26	27
28						

Oh, how I enjoy a good challenge, Lord; and each day challenges me anew! Thank You for these opportunities—for each exciting adventure. My desire is that I might face each task in a godly manner and that I might honor You in all I say and do.

to-do list

- [ ]
- [ ]
- [ ]
- [ ]
- [ ]
- [ ]
- [ ]
- [ ]
- [ ]
- [ ]
- [ ]
- [ ]
- [ ]
- [ ]
- [ ]

SUNDAY, February 14 *Valentine's Day*

MONDAY, February 15 *Presidents' Day*

TUESDAY, February 16

WEDNESDAY, February 17

THURSDAY, February 18

FRIDAY, February 19

SATURDAY, February 20

to-do list

- [ ]
- [ ]
- [ ]
- [ ]
- [ ]
- [ ]
- [ ]
- [ ]
- [ ]
- [ ]
- [ ]
- [ ]
- [ ]
- [ ]
- [ ]
- [ ]

And let us consider how to stir up one another to love and good works, not neglecting to meet together, as is the habit of some, but encouraging one another, and all the more as you see the Day drawing near.

HEBREWS 10:24–25 ESV

February 2027

S	M	T	W	T	F	S
	1	2	3	4	5	6
7	8	9	10	11	12	13
14	15	16	17	18	19	20
21	22	23	24	25	26	27
28						

Lord, often in my daily planning I forget to consult You. Then I wonder why things don't work out the way I think they should. Forgive my arrogant attitude. I know that only as You guide me through the day will I find joy in accomplishments. Show me how to align my goals with Your will.

to-do list

SUNDAY, February 21

MONDAY, February 22

TUESDAY, February 23

WEDNESDAY, February 24

THURSDAY, February 25

FRIDAY, February 26

SATURDAY, February 27

to-do list

- [ ]
- [ ]
- [ ]
- [ ]
- [ ]
- [ ]
- [ ]
- [ ]
- [ ]
- [ ]
- [ ]
- [ ]
- [ ]
- [ ]

But take diligent heed to do the commandment and the law, which Moses the servant of the LORD charged you, to love the LORD your God, and to walk in all his ways, and to keep his commandments, and to cleave unto him, and to serve him with all your heart and with all your soul.

JOSHUA 22:5

March 2027

SUNDAY	MONDAY	TUESDAY	WEDNESDAY
28	1	2	3
7	8	9	10
14 *Daylight Saving Time Begins*	15	16	17 *St. Patrick's Day*
21 *Palm Sunday*	22	23	24
28 *Easter Sunday*	29	30	31

THURSDAY	FRIDAY	SATURDAY
4	5	6
11	12	13
18	19	20 *First Day of Spring*
25	26 *Good Friday*	27
1	2	3

notes

February

S	M	T	W	T	F	S
	1	2	3	4	5	6
7	8	9	10	11	12	13
14	15	16	17	18	19	20
21	22	23	24	25	26	27
28						

April

S	M	T	W	T	F	S
				1	2	3
4	5	6	7	8	9	10
11	12	13	14	15	16	17
18	19	20	21	22	23	24
25	26	27	28	29	30	

Goals for the Month

But I am like an olive tree growing
in God's house, and I can count
on his love forever and ever.
Psalm 52:8 CEV

February–March 2027

S	M	T	W	T	F	S
	1	2	3	4	5	6
7	8	9	10	11	12	13
14	15	16	17	18	19	20
21	22	23	24	25	26	27
28	29	30	31			

Dear God, sometimes godly character sounds so easy to attain when I'm sitting in church, listening to the pastor speak. In my heart I know I want it; in my mind I believe it's possible. Making the ideal become reality is much harder. I need Your strength. Please help me develop godly character.

to-do list

SUNDAY, February 28

MONDAY, March 1

TUESDAY, March 2

WEDNESDAY, March 3

THURSDAY, March 4

FRIDAY, March 5

SATURDAY, March 6

to-do list

Put on then, as God's chosen ones, holy and beloved, compassionate hearts, kindness, humility, meekness. . . . And above all these put on love, which binds everything together in perfect harmony. And let the peace of Christ rule in your hearts, to which indeed you were called in one body. And be thankful.

COLOSSIANS 3:12, 14–15 ESV

March 2027

S	M	T	W	T	F	S
	1	2	3	4	5	6
7	8	9	10	11	12	13
14	15	16	17	18	19	20
21	22	23	24	25	26	27
28	29	30	31			

I have to admit that one of the greatest challenges I face each day is the need for patience. I'm tested regularly on the subject, and too often I fail. Lord, I know I won't win this battle overnight, but with Your help, I'll daily work toward achieving godly patience.

to-do list

- [ ] ....
- [ ] ....
- [ ] ....
- [ ] ....
- [ ] ....
- [ ] ....
- [ ] ....
- [ ] ....
- [ ] ....
- [ ] ....
- [ ] ....
- [ ] ....
- [ ] ....
- [ ] ....
- [ ] ....

SUNDAY, March 7

MONDAY, March 8

TUESDAY, March 9

WEDNESDAY, March 10

THURSDAY, March 11

FRIDAY, March 12

SATURDAY, March 13

to-do list

"Put it in writing, because it is not yet time for it to come true. But the time is coming quickly, and what I show you will come true. It may seem slow in coming, but wait for it; it will certainly take place, and it will not be delayed."

HABAKKUK 2:3 GNT

March 2027

S	M	T	W	T	F	S
	1	2	3	4	5	6
7	8	9	10	11	12	13
14	15	16	17	18	19	20
21	22	23	24	25	26	27
28	29	30	31			

There are many decisions being made on issues concerning our church, Father. They aren't easy decisions to make, and everyone has a different opinion on what the outcome should be. Please give us direction and unity. Work in our midst so that we might bring others into Your kingdom.

to-do list

- [ ]
- [ ]
- [ ]
- [ ]
- [ ]
- [ ]
- [ ]
- [ ]
- [ ]
- [ ]
- [ ]
- [ ]
- [ ]
- [ ]
- [ ]

SUNDAY, March 14 *Daylight Saving Time Begins*

MONDAY, March 15

TUESDAY, March 16

WEDNESDAY, March 17 *St. Patrick's Day*

THURSDAY, March 18

FRIDAY, March 19

SATURDAY, March 20 *First Day of Spring*

to-do list

- [ ]
- [ ]
- [ ]
- [ ]
- [ ]
- [ ]
- [ ]
- [ ]
- [ ]
- [ ]
- [ ]
- [ ]
- [ ]
- [ ]

Do not be anxious about anything, but in everything by prayer and supplication with thanksgiving let your requests be made known to God. And the peace of God, which surpasses all understanding, will guard your hearts and your minds in Christ Jesus.

PHILIPPIANS 4:6–7 ESV

March 2027

S	M	T	W	T	F	S
	1	2	3	4	5	6
7	8	9	10	11	12	13
14	15	16	17	18	19	20
21	22	23	24	25	26	27
28	29	30	31			

Lord, there are so many people in my community who either don't care about You or think they will please You by their own merit; but several of them don't truly know You. I ask You to open doors so I may witness to them. My prayer is that many will come to You.

to-do list

- [ ]
- [ ]
- [ ]
- [ ]
- [ ]
- [ ]
- [ ]
- [ ]
- [ ]
- [ ]
- [ ]
- [ ]
- [ ]
- [ ]
- [ ]

SUNDAY, March 21 *Palm Sunday*

MONDAY, March 22

TUESDAY, March 23

WEDNESDAY, March 24

THURSDAY, March 25

FRIDAY, March 26 *Good Friday*

SATURDAY, March 27

to-do list

"I know your works. Behold, I have set before you an open door, which no one is able to shut. I know that you have but little power, and yet you have kept my word and have not denied my name."

REVELATION 3:8 ESV

April 2027

SUNDAY	MONDAY	TUESDAY	WEDNESDAY
28	29	30	31
4	5	6	7
11	12	13	14
18	19	20	21 *Passover Begins at Sundown*
25	26	27	28

THURSDAY	FRIDAY	SATURDAY
1	2	3
8	9	10
15	16	17
22	23	24
29	30 *Arbor Day*	1

notes

March

S	M	T	W	T	F	S
	1	2	3	4	5	6
7	8	9	10	11	12	13
14	15	16	17	18	19	20
21	22	23	24	25	26	27
28	29	30	31			

May

S	M	T	W	T	F	S
						1
2	3	4	5	6	7	8
9	10	11	12	13	14	15
16	17	18	19	20	21	22
23	24	25	26	27	28	29
30	31					

You,
heavenly
Father,
are my
satisfaction.

Goals for the Month

[God,] I'm leaping and singing in the circle of your love.

PSALM 31:7 MSG

March–April 2027

S	M	T	W	T	F	S
				1	2	3
4	5	6	7	8	9	10
11	12	13	14	15	16	17
18	19	20	21	22	23	24
25	26	27	28	29	30	

One of the most interesting stories in Your Word is about the time You cleansed the temple, Father. It has taught me that there is a time and place for anger. Sin is always something that should evoke fury. Just help me to direct my anger at the sin and not the sinner.

to-do list

- [ ]
- [ ]
- [ ]
- [ ]
- [ ]
- [ ]
- [ ]
- [ ]
- [ ]
- [ ]
- [ ]
- [ ]
- [ ]
- [ ]
- [ ]

SUNDAY, March 28 *Easter Sunday*

MONDAY, March 29

TUESDAY, March 30

WEDNESDAY, March 31

THURSDAY, April 1

FRIDAY, April 2

SATURDAY, April 3

to-do list

My dear brothers and sisters, take note of this: Everyone should be quick to listen, slow to speak and slow to become angry, because human anger does not produce the righteousness that God desires.

JAMES 1:19–20 NIV

April 2027

S	M	T	W	T	F	S
				1	2	3
4	5	6	7	8	9	10
11	12	13	14	15	16	17
18	19	20	21	22	23	24
25	26	27	28	29	30	

Life's challenge—how can I describe it? I might say it is my best-laid plans peppered with interruptions, broken equipment, lack of sleep, and the necessity to complete a task in the allotted amount of time regardless of the circumstances. It sounds rough, and it often seems that way; but with Your help, Father God, I can endure!

to-do list

- [ ]
- [ ]
- [ ]
- [ ]
- [ ]
- [ ]
- [ ]
- [ ]
- [ ]
- [ ]
- [ ]
- [ ]
- [ ]
- [ ]
- [ ]

SUNDAY, April 4

MONDAY, April 5

TUESDAY, April 6

WEDNESDAY, April 7

THURSDAY, April 8

FRIDAY, April 9

SATURDAY, April 10

to-do list

- [ ]
- [ ]
- [ ]
- [ ]
- [ ]
- [ ]
- [ ]
- [ ]
- [ ]
- [ ]
- [ ]
- [ ]
- [ ]
- [ ]
- [ ]
- [ ]

[Love] beareth all things, believeth all things, hopeth all things, endureth all things.
1 CORINTHIANS 13:7

April 2027

S	M	T	W	T	F	S
				1	2	3
4	5	6	7	8	9	10
11	12	13	14	15	16	17
18	19	20	21	22	23	24
25	26	27	28	29	30	

Lord, how alone You must have been in the garden when the disciples fell asleep. And when God turned His back as You hung on the cross—was there anything to compare to what You felt? Yet You did it willingly. You understand when I'm lonely, and I thank You for being there during those times.

to-do list

- [ ]
- [ ]
- [ ]
- [ ]
- [ ]
- [ ]
- [ ]
- [ ]
- [ ]
- [ ]
- [ ]
- [ ]
- [ ]
- [ ]
- [ ]

SUNDAY, April 11

MONDAY, April 12

TUESDAY, April 13

WEDNESDAY, April 14

THURSDAY, April 15

FRIDAY, April 16

SATURDAY, April 17

to-do list

"I've called your name.
You're mine."
ISAIAH 43:1 MSG

April 2027

S	M	T	W	T	F	S
				1	2	3
4	5	6	7	8	9	10
11	12	13	14	15	16	17
18	19	20	21	22	23	24
25	26	27	28	29	30	

Sometimes I get so frustrated, Lord. I've asked what You want from me, but it seems You've remained silent. Then I realize that there are specifics in Your Word that I should automatically be doing. I haven't always been obedient in those, so how can I expect to know more? Forgive me, Father. I want to obey.

to-do list

- [ ]
- [ ]
- [ ]
- [ ]
- [ ]
- [ ]
- [ ]
- [ ]
- [ ]
- [ ]
- [ ]
- [ ]
- [ ]
- [ ]
- [ ]

SUNDAY, April 18

MONDAY, April 19

TUESDAY, April 20

WEDNESDAY, April 21 *Passover Begins at Sundown*

THURSDAY, April 22

FRIDAY, April 23

SATURDAY, April 24

to-do list

Jesus said unto him,
Thou shalt love the Lord
thy God with all thy heart,
and with all thy soul,
and with all thy mind.
MATTHEW 22:37

April–May 2027

S	M	T	W	T	F	S
				1	2	3
4	5	6	7	8	9	10
11	12	13	14	15	16	17
18	19	20	21	22	23	24
25	26	27	28	29	30	

Lord, we sometimes sing a song about being happy because You took our burdens all away. I guess You really just make the burdens more bearable. Still, that's something great to sing about, and it does bring happiness. I'm so glad You're there to lighten the load.

to-do list

- [ ]
- [ ]
- [ ]
- [ ]
- [ ]
- [ ]
- [ ]
- [ ]
- [ ]
- [ ]
- [ ]
- [ ]
- [ ]
- [ ]
- [ ]

SUNDAY, April 25

MONDAY, April 26

TUESDAY, April 27

WEDNESDAY, April 28

THURSDAY, April 29

FRIDAY, April 30 *Arbor Day*

SATURDAY, May 1

to-do list

O come, let us sing unto the LORD: let us make a joyful noise to the rock of our salvation. Let us come before his presence with thanksgiving, and make a joyful noise unto him with psalms.
PSALM 95:1–2

May 2027

SUNDAY	MONDAY	TUESDAY	WEDNESDAY
25	26	27	28
2	3	4	5
9 *Mother's Day*	10	11	12
16	17	18	19
23 / 30	24 / 31 *Memorial Day*	25	26

THURSDAY	FRIDAY	SATURDAY
29	30	1
6 *National Day of Prayer*	7	8
13	14	15
20	21	22
27	28	29

notes

April

S	M	T	W	T	F	S
				1	2	3
4	5	6	7	8	9	10
11	12	13	14	15	16	17
18	19	20	21	22	23	24
25	26	27	28	29	30	

June

S	M	T	W	T	F	S
		1	2	3	4	5
6	7	8	9	10	11	12
13	14	15	16	17	18	19
20	21	22	23	24	25	26
27	28	29	30			

Goals for the Month

On your feet now—applaud
God! Bring a gift of laughter,
sing yourselves into his presence.
Psalm 100:1–2 msg

May 2027

S	M	T	W	T	F	S
						1
2	3	4	5	6	7	8
9	10	11	12	13	14	15
16	17	18	19	20	21	22
23	24	25	26	27	28	29
30	31					

Lord, let my home be a comforting haven for my family and friends. May it be a place where they can momentarily escape the pressures of this world. Help me to do my best to make it a place where people will know they are loved by me and, more importantly, by You.

to-do list

- [ ]
- [ ]
- [ ]
- [ ]
- [ ]
- [ ]
- [ ]
- [ ]
- [ ]
- [ ]
- [ ]
- [ ]
- [ ]
- [ ]
- [ ]

SUNDAY, May 2

MONDAY, May 3

TUESDAY, May 4

WEDNESDAY, May 5

THURSDAY, May 6 *National Day of Prayer*

FRIDAY, May 7

SATURDAY, May 8

to-do list

This is my commandment, That ye love one another, as I have loved you.
JOHN 15:12

May 2027

S	M	T	W	T	F	S
						1
2	3	4	5	6	7	8
9	10	11	12	13	14	15
16	17	18	19	20	21	22
23	24	25	26	27	28	29
30	31					

Love—what a beautiful word! Yet many people are so cynical about it, dear Jesus. I guess that's because there is so much artificial affection in this world, but I'd like for people to see true love—Your love—in my life. Please give me the ability to love as You do.

to-do list

- [ ]
- [ ]
- [ ]
- [ ]
- [ ]
- [ ]
- [ ]
- [ ]
- [ ]
- [ ]
- [ ]
- [ ]
- [ ]
- [ ]
- [ ]

SUNDAY, May 9 *Mother's Day*

MONDAY, May 10

TUESDAY, May 11

WEDNESDAY, May 12

THURSDAY, May 13

FRIDAY, May 14

SATURDAY, May 15

to-do list

- [ ]
- [ ]
- [ ]
- [ ]
- [ ]
- [ ]
- [ ]
- [ ]
- [ ]
- [ ]
- [ ]
- [ ]
- [ ]
- [ ]
- [ ]
- [ ]

But God, who is rich in mercy, for his great love wherewith he loved us, even when we were dead in sins, hath quickened us together with Christ.

EPHESIANS 2:4–5

May 2027

S	M	T	W	T	F	S
						1
2	3	4	5	6	7	8
9	10	11	12	13	14	15
16	17	18	19	20	21	22
23	24	25	26	27	28	29
30	31					

Jesus, others, you. What a simple yet profound way to achieve joy. And I'm beginning to see just how much this really works. I guess that's because when You are first in my life, everything else is properly prioritized. Although putting others before myself isn't always easy, it feels wonderful when I do it.

to-do list

- [ ]
- [ ]
- [ ]
- [ ]
- [ ]
- [ ]
- [ ]
- [ ]
- [ ]
- [ ]
- [ ]
- [ ]
- [ ]
- [ ]
- [ ]

SUNDAY, May 16

MONDAY, May 17

TUESDAY, May 18

WEDNESDAY, May 19

THURSDAY, May 20

FRIDAY, May 21

SATURDAY, May 22

to-do list

Do nothing from selfish ambition or conceit, but in humility count others more significant than yourselves.

PHILIPPIANS 2:3 ESV

May 2027

S	M	T	W	T	F	S
						1
2	3	4	5	6	7	8
9	10	11	12	13	14	15
16	17	18	19	20	21	22
23	24	25	26	27	28	29
30	31					

In Your Word, You've commanded us to take the gospel to all nations. You've also said that when we're obedient, You'll meet our needs. Please meet the needs of our missionaries, Lord. Provide what they need physically and spiritually, and let many souls be saved as a result.

to-do list

- [ ]
- [ ]
- [ ]
- [ ]
- [ ]
- [ ]
- [ ]
- [ ]
- [ ]
- [ ]
- [ ]
- [ ]
- [ ]
- [ ]
- [ ]

SUNDAY, May 23

MONDAY, May 24

TUESDAY, May 25

WEDNESDAY, May 26

THURSDAY, May 27

FRIDAY, May 28

SATURDAY, May 29

to-do list

But my God shall supply all your need according to his riches in glory by Christ Jesus.

PHILIPPIANS 4:19

June 2027

SUNDAY	MONDAY	TUESDAY	WEDNESDAY
30	31	1	2
6	7	8	9
13	14 *Flag Day*	15	16
20 *Father's Day*	21 *First Day of Summer*	22	23
27	28	29	30

THURSDAY	FRIDAY	SATURDAY
3	4	5
10	11	12
17	18	19 *Juneteenth*
24	25	26
1	2	3

notes

May

S	M	T	W	T	F	S
						1
2	3	4	5	6	7	8
9	10	11	12	13	14	15
16	17	18	19	20	21	22
23	24	25	26	27	28	29
30	31					

July

S	M	T	W	T	F	S
				1	2	3
4	5	6	7	8	9	10
11	12	13	14	15	16	17
18	19	20	21	22	23	24
25	26	27	28	29	30	31

Goals for the Month

I run in the path of your commands, for you have broadened my understanding.
Psalm 119:32 NIV

May–June 2027

S	M	T	W	T	F	S
		1	2	3	4	5
6	7	8	9	10	11	12
13	14	15	16	17	18	19
20	21	22	23	24	25	26
27	28	29	30			

Dear God, I was just noticing all the people around me who really could use a friend. For whatever reason, they're alone and hurting. I need to reach out to them. I ask You to give me opportunities and ideas to let them know I care. Let me make the world a little friendlier for them.

to-do list

- [ ]
- [ ]
- [ ]
- [ ]
- [ ]
- [ ]
- [ ]
- [ ]
- [ ]
- [ ]
- [ ]
- [ ]
- [ ]
- [ ]
- [ ]

SUNDAY, May 30

MONDAY, May 31 *Memorial Day*

TUESDAY, June 1

WEDNESDAY, June 2

THURSDAY, June 3

FRIDAY, June 4

SATURDAY, June 5

to-do list

- [ ]
- [ ]
- [ ]
- [ ]
- [ ]
- [ ]
- [ ]
- [ ]
- [ ]
- [ ]
- [ ]
- [ ]
- [ ]
- [ ]
- [ ]
- [ ]

And he said unto them,
Go ye into all the world,
and preach the gospel
to every creature.
MARK 16:15

June 2027

S	M	T	W	T	F	S
		1	2	3	4	5
6	7	8	9	10	11	12
13	14	15	16	17	18	19
20	21	22	23	24	25	26
27	28	29	30			

I say I love You, Father, although I'm not sure it goes as deep as it should. I want it to, though. I want to be so in love with You that it shows in every aspect of my life. Help me to develop the intimacy with You that I should have.

to-do list

- [ ]
- [ ]
- [ ]
- [ ]
- [ ]
- [ ]
- [ ]
- [ ]
- [ ]
- [ ]
- [ ]
- [ ]
- [ ]
- [ ]
- [ ]

SUNDAY, June 6

MONDAY, June 7

TUESDAY, June 8

WEDNESDAY, June 9

THURSDAY, June 10

FRIDAY, June 11

SATURDAY, June 12

to-do list

- [ ]
- [ ]
- [ ]
- [ ]
- [ ]
- [ ]
- [ ]
- [ ]
- [ ]
- [ ]
- [ ]
- [ ]
- [ ]
- [ ]
- [ ]
- [ ]

"You shall love the Lord your God with all your heart and with all your soul and with all your mind."

MATTHEW 22:37 ESV

June 2027

S	M	T	W	T	F	S
		1	2	3	4	5
6	7	8	9	10	11	12
13	14	15	16	17	18	19
20	21	22	23	24	25	26
27	28	29	30			

So many people think that modesty is only a clothing issue, but You've shown me that it's so much more. It's an attitude akin to humility, and it's what You want from me. Even in this You set the example for me, Jesus. Help me to follow the pattern You've given me.

to-do list

- [ ] ....
- [ ] ....
- [ ] ....
- [ ] ....
- [ ] ....
- [ ] ....
- [ ] ....
- [ ] ....
- [ ] ....
- [ ] ....
- [ ] ....
- [ ] ....
- [ ] ....
- [ ] ....
- [ ] ....

SUNDAY, June 13

MONDAY, June 14 *Flag Day*

TUESDAY, June 15

WEDNESDAY, June 16

THURSDAY, June 17

FRIDAY, June 18

SATURDAY, June 19 *Juneteenth*

to-do list

- [ ]
- [ ]
- [ ]
- [ ]
- [ ]
- [ ]
- [ ]
- [ ]
- [ ]
- [ ]
- [ ]
- [ ]
- [ ]
- [ ]
- [ ]

In like manner also, that women adorn themselves in modest apparel, with shamefacedness and sobriety; not with broided hair, or gold, or pearls, or costly array; but (which becometh women professing godliness) with good works.

1 Timothy 2:9–10

June 2027

S	M	T	W	T	F	S
		1	2	3	4	5
6	7	8	9	10	11	12
13	14	15	16	17	18	19
20	21	22	23	24	25	26
27	28	29	30			

I guess we all like to receive praise from time to time, and in moderation it's probably good for us. But, Father, give me a modest heart about the honor when it does come. Don't let me become puffed with pride. I want to give the glory to You, for without You I am nothing.

to-do list

- [ ]
- [ ]
- [ ]
- [ ]
- [ ]
- [ ]
- [ ]
- [ ]
- [ ]
- [ ]
- [ ]
- [ ]
- [ ]
- [ ]
- [ ]

SUNDAY, June 20 *Father's Day*

MONDAY, June 21 *First Day of Summer*

TUESDAY, June 22

WEDNESDAY, June 23

THURSDAY, June 24

FRIDAY, June 25

SATURDAY, June 26

to-do list

But let it be the hidden man of the heart, in that which is not corruptible, even the ornament of a meek and quiet spirit, which is in the sight of God of great price.

1 Peter 3:4

July 2027

SUNDAY	MONDAY	TUESDAY	WEDNESDAY
27	28	29	30
4 *Independence Day*	5	6	7
11	12	13	14
18	19	20	21
25	26	27	28

THURSDAY	FRIDAY	SATURDAY
1	2	3
8	9	10
15	16	17
22	23	24
29	30	31

notes

June

S	M	T	W	T	F	S
		1	2	3	4	5
6	7	8	9	10	11	12
13	14	15	16	17	18	19
20	21	22	23	24	25	26
27	28	29	30			

August

S	M	T	W	T	F	S
1	2	3	4	5	6	7
8	9	10	11	12	13	14
15	16	17	18	19	20	21
22	23	24	25	26	27	28
29	30	31				

Sustain Me, Lord,
with the power of
Your love.

Goals for the Month

You will eat the fruit of your labor; blessings and prosperity will be yours.
Psalm 128:2 NIV

June–July 2027

S	M	T	W	T	F	S
				1	2	3
4	5	6	7	8	9	10
11	12	13	14	15	16	17
18	19	20	21	22	23	24
25	26	27	28	29	30	31

How beautiful to watch a sleeping child! With an arm wrapped gently around his teddy bear and his thumb in his mouth, he embodies peacefulness. As I watch him, I am reminded that You've promised peaceful rest to those in Your care. Oh, how I thank You for this!

to-do list

- [ ]
- [ ]
- [ ]
- [ ]
- [ ]
- [ ]
- [ ]
- [ ]
- [ ]
- [ ]
- [ ]
- [ ]
- [ ]
- [ ]
- [ ]

SUNDAY, June 27

MONDAY, June 28

TUESDAY, June 29

WEDNESDAY, June 30

THURSDAY, July 1

FRIDAY, July 2

SATURDAY, July 3

to-do list

Take my yoke upon you, and learn of me; for I am meek and lowly in heart: and ye shall find rest unto your souls.

MATTHEW 11:29

July 2027

S	M	T	W	T	F	S
				1	2	3
4	5	6	7	8	9	10
11	12	13	14	15	16	17
18	19	20	21	22	23	24
25	26	27	28	29	30	31

I really didn't want to get up this morning, Father. My blankets seemed like good protection from the cares of the day. But when I saw the glorious sunrise and heard the cheerful, singing birds, I was reminded that Your compassions are new every morning. I knew everything would be fine. Thank You for Your faithfulness.

to-do list

- [ ]
- [ ]
- [ ]
- [ ]
- [ ]
- [ ]
- [ ]
- [ ]
- [ ]
- [ ]
- [ ]
- [ ]
- [ ]
- [ ]
- [ ]

SUNDAY, July 4 *Independence Day*

MONDAY, July 5

TUESDAY, July 6

WEDNESDAY, July 7

THURSDAY, July 8

FRIDAY, July 9

SATURDAY, July 10

to-do list

It is of the L*ORD's mercies that we are not consumed, because his compassions fail not. They are new every morning: great is thy faithfulness.*

LAMENTATIONS 3:22–23

July 2027

S	M	T	W	T	F	S
				1	2	3
4	5	6	7	8	9	10
11	12	13	14	15	16	17
18	19	20	21	22	23	24
25	26	27	28	29	30	31

It's a fast-paced world where everyone wants to get ahead, Father. Sometimes contentment is frowned upon. Some folks think of it as laziness or lack of motivation. But I know that if I am in the center of Your will, I'll be content. That's the only true contentment there is.

to-do list

- [ ]
- [ ]
- [ ]
- [ ]
- [ ]
- [ ]
- [ ]
- [ ]
- [ ]
- [ ]
- [ ]
- [ ]
- [ ]
- [ ]
- [ ]

SUNDAY, July 11

MONDAY, July 12

TUESDAY, July 13

WEDNESDAY, July 14

THURSDAY, July 15

FRIDAY, July 16

SATURDAY, July 17

to-do list

I know that there is nothing better for people than to be happy and to do good while they live. That each of them may eat and drink, and find satisfaction in all their toil—this is the gift of God.
ECCLESIASTES 3:12–13 NIV

July 2027

S	M	T	W	T	F	S
				1	2	3
4	5	6	7	8	9	10
11	12	13	14	15	16	17
18	19	20	21	22	23	24
25	26	27	28	29	30	31

It doesn't take much to please a kitten, does it, Lord? Put him on my lap, rub his head, and listen to him purr. What contentment! I wish I were like that, but it seems the more I gain, the more I strive for. There's not much contentment in that. Let me learn from the cat to be satisfied no matter what!

to-do list

- [ ]
- [ ]
- [ ]
- [ ]
- [ ]
- [ ]
- [ ]
- [ ]
- [ ]
- [ ]
- [ ]
- [ ]
- [ ]
- [ ]
- [ ]

SUNDAY, July 18

MONDAY, July 19

TUESDAY, July 20

WEDNESDAY, July 21

THURSDAY, July 22

FRIDAY, July 23

SATURDAY, July 24

to-do list

- [ ]
- [ ]
- [ ]
- [ ]
- [ ]
- [ ]
- [ ]
- [ ]
- [ ]
- [ ]
- [ ]
- [ ]
- [ ]
- [ ]
- [ ]
- [ ]

But godliness with contentment is great gain.
1 TIMOTHY 6:6

July 2027

S	M	T	W	T	F	S
				1	2	3
4	5	6	7	8	9	10
11	12	13	14	15	16	17
18	19	20	21	22	23	24
25	26	27	28	29	30	31

Sometimes my attitude is so "poor me" that I even get sick, Father. I keep thinking that if only I could have this or that, life would be easier. I know I'm missing out on a truly abundant life by whining so much, and I ask You to forgive me. Fill me with contentment.

to-do list

- [ ]
- [ ]
- [ ]
- [ ]
- [ ]
- [ ]
- [ ]
- [ ]
- [ ]
- [ ]
- [ ]
- [ ]
- [ ]
- [ ]
- [ ]

SUNDAY, July 25

MONDAY, July 26

TUESDAY, July 27

WEDNESDAY, July 28

THURSDAY, July 29

FRIDAY, July 30

SATURDAY, July 31

to-do list

Take heed, and beware of covetousness: for a man's life consisteth not in the abundance of the things which he possesseth.

LUKE 12:15

August 2027

SUNDAY	MONDAY	TUESDAY	WEDNESDAY
1	2	3	4
8	9	10	11
15	16	17	18
22	23	24	25
29	30	31	1

THURSDAY	FRIDAY	SATURDAY
5	6	7
12	13	14
19	20	21
26	27	28
2	3	4

notes

July

S	M	T	W	T	F	S
				1	2	3
4	5	6	7	8	9	10
11	12	13	14	15	16	17
18	19	20	21	22	23	24
25	26	27	28	29	30	31

September

S	M	T	W	T	F	S
			1	2	3	4
5	6	7	8	9	10	11
12	13	14	15	16	17	18
19	20	21	22	23	24	25
26	27	28	29	30		

Goals for the Month

Show me the right path,
O Lord; point out the
road for me to follow.
Psalm 25:4 NLT

August 2027

S	M	T	W	T	F	S
1	2	3	4	5	6	7
8	9	10	11	12	13	14
15	16	17	18	19	20	21
22	23	24	25	26	27	28
29	30	31				

I am exhausted, Lord, but I don't think I've ever felt better! There's nothing quite like a hard day's work to bring a tremendous amount of satisfaction. And I'm really anticipating the good night's sleep ahead because I know I pleased You with my effort today.

to-do list

SUNDAY, August 1

MONDAY, August 2

TUESDAY, August 3

WEDNESDAY, August 4

THURSDAY, August 5

FRIDAY, August 6

SATURDAY, August 7

to-do list

- [ ]
- [ ]
- [ ]
- [ ]
- [ ]
- [ ]
- [ ]
- [ ]
- [ ]
- [ ]
- [ ]
- [ ]
- [ ]
- [ ]
- [ ]
- [ ]

Give her of the fruit of her hands; and let her own works praise her in the gates.
PROVERBS 31:31

August 2027

S	M	T	W	T	F	S
1	2	3	4	5	6	7
8	9	10	11	12	13	14
15	16	17	18	19	20	21
22	23	24	25	26	27	28
29	30	31				

I am convinced, Father, that one reason You bring children across our paths is to teach us important lessons. It wasn't long ago that I heard a small child thanking You for many things. "And thank You for the lightning bugs," he said. What a simple reminder that there's nothing too insignificant for which to offer thanks.

to-do list

- [ ]
- [ ]
- [ ]
- [ ]
- [ ]
- [ ]
- [ ]
- [ ]
- [ ]
- [ ]
- [ ]
- [ ]
- [ ]
- [ ]
- [ ]

SUNDAY, August 8

MONDAY, August 9

TUESDAY, August 10

WEDNESDAY, August 11

THURSDAY, August 12

FRIDAY, August 13

SATURDAY, August 14

to-do list

Oh that men would praise the L*ORD* *for his goodness, and for his wonderful works to the children of men!*

PSALM 107:8

August 2027

S	M	T	W	T	F	S
1	2	3	4	5	6	7
8	9	10	11	12	13	14
15	16	17	18	19	20	21
22	23	24	25	26	27	28
29	30	31				

Among Your many blessings, my family ranks near the top. They share my joys and help bear my burdens. Dear Jesus, I know that You selected each of my relatives to be a part of my life in a special way, and I thank You for each of them. May I bring happiness to them in some way too!

to-do list

- [ ]
- [ ]
- [ ]
- [ ]
- [ ]
- [ ]
- [ ]
- [ ]
- [ ]
- [ ]
- [ ]
- [ ]
- [ ]
- [ ]
- [ ]

SUNDAY, August 15

MONDAY, August 16

TUESDAY, August 17

WEDNESDAY, August 18

THURSDAY, August 19

FRIDAY, August 20

SATURDAY, August 21

to-do list

And if it seem evil unto you
to serve the LORD, *choose you*
this day whom ye will serve;
whether the gods which your
fathers served that were on
the other side of the flood,
or the gods of the Amorites,
in whose land ye dwell:
but as for me and my house,
we will serve the LORD.

JOSHUA 24:15

August 2027

S	M	T	W	T	F	S
1	2	3	4	5	6	7
8	9	10	11	12	13	14
15	16	17	18	19	20	21
22	23	24	25	26	27	28
29	30	31				

Father, please show me if the life I live is truly pure in Your sight. In my pride, I'm afraid I raise myself to greater heights than I ought to where cleanliness is involved. But I want to see myself through Your eyes. I want to measure up to Your standards. Please purify my attitude, Lord.

to-do list

- [ ]
- [ ]
- [ ]
- [ ]
- [ ]
- [ ]
- [ ]
- [ ]
- [ ]
- [ ]
- [ ]
- [ ]
- [ ]
- [ ]
- [ ]

SUNDAY, August 22

MONDAY, August 23

TUESDAY, August 24

WEDNESDAY, August 25

THURSDAY, August 26

FRIDAY, August 27

SATURDAY, August 28

to-do list

Blessed are the pure in heart:
for they shall see God.
Matthew 5:8

September 2027

SUNDAY	MONDAY	TUESDAY	WEDNESDAY
29	30	31	1
5	6 *Labor Day*	7	8
12	13	14	15
19	20	21	22 *See You at the Pole*
26	27	28	29

THURSDAY	FRIDAY	SATURDAY
2	3	4
9	10	11
16	17	18
23 *First Day of Autumn*	24	25
30	1	2

notes

August

S	M	T	W	T	F	S
1	2	3	4	5	6	7
8	9	10	11	12	13	14
15	16	17	18	19	20	21
22	23	24	25	26	27	28
29	30	31				

October

S	M	T	W	T	F	S
					1	2
3	4	5	6	7	8	9
10	11	12	13	14	15	16
17	18	19	20	21	22	23
24	25	26	27	28	29	30
31						

I need your
healing and
peace
Lord.

Goals for the Month

And the Lord will deliver me from every evil work and preserve me for His heavenly kingdom. To Him be glory forever and ever. Amen!
2 Timothy 4:18 NKJV

August–September 2027

S	M	T	W	T	F	S
			1	2	3	4
5	6	7	8	9	10	11
12	13	14	15	16	17	18
19	20	21	22	23	24	25
26	27	28	29	30		

It's funny, Lord. It seems like I always wish I had more money, but dealing with it can sometimes be a pain. Keeping it organized, making sure my bills are paid—at times it's overwhelming. Please give me a clear mind and wisdom to handle my financial responsibilities according to Your will.

to-do list

- [ ]
- [ ]
- [ ]
- [ ]
- [ ]
- [ ]
- [ ]
- [ ]
- [ ]
- [ ]
- [ ]
- [ ]
- [ ]
- [ ]
- [ ]

SUNDAY, August 29

MONDAY, August 30

TUESDAY, August 31

WEDNESDAY, September 1

THURSDAY, September 2

FRIDAY, September 3

SATURDAY, September 4

to-do list

- [ ]
- [ ]
- [ ]
- [ ]
- [ ]
- [ ]
- [ ]
- [ ]
- [ ]
- [ ]
- [ ]
- [ ]
- [ ]
- [ ]
- [ ]
- [ ]

But seek ye first the kingdom of God, and his righteousness; and all these things shall be added unto you.

MATTHEW 6:33

September 2027

S	M	T	W	T	F	S
			1	2	3	4
5	6	7	8	9	10	11
12	13	14	15	16	17	18
19	20	21	22	23	24	25
26	27	28	29	30		

I know that You've brought people into my life for many different reasons, but I have to admit that sometimes I'd like to take my dog and move to my own island. It's hard to please people, and it's easy to upset them. Neither situation is pleasant for me. Lord, please help me do my best in each relationship.

to-do list

- [ ]
- [ ]
- [ ]
- [ ]
- [ ]
- [ ]
- [ ]
- [ ]
- [ ]
- [ ]
- [ ]
- [ ]
- [ ]
- [ ]
- [ ]

SUNDAY, September 5

MONDAY, September 6 *Labor Day*

TUESDAY, September 7

WEDNESDAY, September 8

THURSDAY, September 9

FRIDAY, September 10

SATURDAY, September 11

to-do list

- [ ]
- [ ]
- [ ]
- [ ]
- [ ]
- [ ]
- [ ]
- [ ]
- [ ]
- [ ]
- [ ]
- [ ]
- [ ]
- [ ]
- [ ]
- [ ]

And let us consider one
another to provoke unto
love and to good works:
not forsaking the assembling
of ourselves together,
as the manner of some is;
but exhorting one another:
and so much the more, as ye
see the day approaching.

HEBREWS 10:24–25

September 2027

S	M	T	W	T	F	S
			1	2	3	4
5	6	7	8	9	10	11
12	13	14	15	16	17	18
19	20	21	22	23	24	25
26	27	28	29	30		

I've been concentrating so much on my grief, Lord, that I'm afraid my perspective of You has become warped. I wonder why You allow bad things to happen, and sometimes I even question whether or not You really love me. I know the truth is that You are right there with me, wanting me to trust and love You more. Help me keep that in focus.

to-do list

- [ ]
- [ ]
- [ ]
- [ ]
- [ ]
- [ ]
- [ ]
- [ ]
- [ ]
- [ ]
- [ ]
- [ ]
- [ ]
- [ ]
- [ ]

SUNDAY, September 12

MONDAY, September 13

TUESDAY, September 14

WEDNESDAY, September 15

THURSDAY, September 16

FRIDAY, September 17

SATURDAY, September 18

to-do list

For I am persuaded that neither death nor life, nor angels nor principalities nor powers, nor things present nor things to come, nor height nor depth, nor any other created thing, shall be able to separate us from the love of God which is in Christ Jesus our Lord.

ROMANS 8:38–39 NKJV

September 2027

S	M	T	W	T	F	S
			1	2	3	4
5	6	7	8	9	10	11
12	13	14	15	16	17	18
19	20	21	22	23	24	25
26	27	28	29	30		

A lot of times I've heard people say that Christians can be joyful without being happy, and I know that's true. Still, I relish those happy times in life. It feels good to laugh so hard that I'm crying and to smile because I see something cute. Thank You for giving me happy times to enjoy, dear Jesus.

to-do list

- [ ] ....
- [ ] ....
- [ ] ....
- [ ] ....
- [ ] ....
- [ ] ....
- [ ] ....
- [ ] ....
- [ ] ....
- [ ] ....
- [ ] ....
- [ ] ....
- [ ] ....
- [ ] ....
- [ ] ....

SUNDAY, September 19

MONDAY, September 20

TUESDAY, September 21

WEDNESDAY, September 22 *See You at the Pole*

THURSDAY, September 23 *First Day of Autumn*

FRIDAY, September 24

SATURDAY, September 25

to-do list

- [ ]
- [ ]
- [ ]
- [ ]
- [ ]
- [ ]
- [ ]
- [ ]
- [ ]
- [ ]
- [ ]
- [ ]
- [ ]
- [ ]
- [ ]
- [ ]

This is the day that the LORD *has made; let us rejoice and be glad in it.*
PSALM 118:24 ESV

October 2027

SUNDAY	MONDAY	TUESDAY	WEDNESDAY
26	27	28	29
3	4	5	6
10	11 *Columbus Day*	12	13
17	18	19	20
24 / *Halloween* 31	25	26	27

THURSDAY	FRIDAY	SATURDAY
30	1	2
7	8	9
14	15	16
21	22	23
28	29	30

notes

September

S	M	T	W	T	F	S
			1	2	3	4
5	6	7	8	9	10	11
12	13	14	15	16	17	18
19	20	21	22	23	24	25
26	27	28	29	30		

November

S	M	T	W	T	F	S
	1	2	3	4	5	6
7	8	9	10	11	12	13
14	15	16	17	18	19	20
21	22	23	24	25	26	27
28	29	30				

Goals for the Month

"But when you pray, go away by yourself, shut the door behind you, and pray to your Father in private. Then your Father, who sees everything, will reward you."
MATTHEW 6:6 NLT

September–October 2027

S	M	T	W	T	F	S
					1	2
3	4	5	6	7	8	9
10	11	12	13	14	15	16
17	18	19	20	21	22	23
24	25	26	27	28	29	30
31						

Do You feel welcome in my home, Father? Are You happy to be here, or are You ashamed to call me Your child? I want You to be more important in our daily lives than anything else, and I want to open our home to You to use in any way You choose.

to-do list

- [ ]
- [ ]
- [ ]
- [ ]
- [ ]
- [ ]
- [ ]
- [ ]
- [ ]
- [ ]
- [ ]
- [ ]
- [ ]
- [ ]
- [ ]

SUNDAY, September 26

MONDAY, September 27

TUESDAY, September 28

WEDNESDAY, September 29

THURSDAY, September 30

FRIDAY, October 1

SATURDAY, October 2

to-do list

- [ ]
- [ ]
- [ ]
- [ ]
- [ ]
- [ ]
- [ ]
- [ ]
- [ ]
- [ ]
- [ ]
- [ ]
- [ ]
- [ ]
- [ ]
- [ ]

Study to shew thyself approved unto God, a workman that needeth not to be ashamed, rightly dividing the word of truth.

2 Timothy 2:15

October 2027

S	M	T	W	T	F	S
					1	2
3	4	5	6	7	8	9
10	11	12	13	14	15	16
17	18	19	20	21	22	23
24	25	26	27	28	29	30
31						

We're by nature very proud, Jesus. Humility certainly doesn't come easily. But You are humble, and You are the example I am to follow regardless of what comes readily. Teach me to be more like You. Teach me to be a servant.

to-do list

- [ ]
- [ ]
- [ ]
- [ ]
- [ ]
- [ ]
- [ ]
- [ ]
- [ ]
- [ ]
- [ ]
- [ ]
- [ ]
- [ ]
- [ ]

SUNDAY, October 3

MONDAY, October 4

TUESDAY, October 5

WEDNESDAY, October 6

THURSDAY, October 7

FRIDAY, October 8

SATURDAY, October 9

to-do list

- [ ]
- [ ]
- [ ]
- [ ]
- [ ]
- [ ]
- [ ]
- [ ]
- [ ]
- [ ]
- [ ]
- [ ]
- [ ]
- [ ]
- [ ]
- [ ]

Look upon me with love;
teach me your decrees.
PSALM 119:135 NLT

October 2027

S	M	T	W	T	F	S
					1	2
3	4	5	6	7	8	9
10	11	12	13	14	15	16
17	18	19	20	21	22	23
24	25	26	27	28	29	30
31						

I love listening to children singing songs about joy. They're such positive tunes, and I find myself wanting to join in. And why shouldn't I? I'm sure it would please You to hear adults belting out these joyful Sunday school verses with as much conviction as the little ones. After all, You've given us our joy.

to-do list

- [ ] ....
- [ ] ....
- [ ] ....
- [ ] ....
- [ ] ....
- [ ] ....
- [ ] ....
- [ ] ....
- [ ] ....
- [ ] ....
- [ ] ....
- [ ] ....
- [ ] ....
- [ ] ....
- [ ] ....

SUNDAY, October 10

MONDAY, October 11

Columbus Day

TUESDAY, October 12

WEDNESDAY, October 13

THURSDAY, October 14

FRIDAY, October 15

SATURDAY, October 16

to-do list

Whom having not seen,
ye love; in whom, though
now ye see him not, yet
believing, ye rejoice with joy
unspeakable and full of glory.
1 PETER 1:8

October 2027

S	M	T	W	T	F	S
					1	2
3	4	5	6	7	8	9
10	11	12	13	14	15	16
17	18	19	20	21	22	23
24	25	26	27	28	29	30
31						

There are many people in my family who have not accepted Your gift of salvation, dear Jesus. My most heartfelt prayer for each of them is that they will trust You. Draw each of them into Your embrace. I pray that each would receive You as Savior.

to-do list

- [ ]
- [ ]
- [ ]
- [ ]
- [ ]
- [ ]
- [ ]
- [ ]
- [ ]
- [ ]
- [ ]
- [ ]
- [ ]
- [ ]
- [ ]

SUNDAY, October 17

MONDAY, October 18

TUESDAY, October 19

WEDNESDAY, October 20

THURSDAY, October 21

FRIDAY, October 22

SATURDAY, October 23

to-do list

For God so loved the world,
that he gave his only begotten
Son, that whosoever believeth
in him should not perish,
but have everlasting life.
JOHN 3:16

October 2027

S	M	T	W	T	F	S
					1	2
3	4	5	6	7	8	9
10	11	12	13	14	15	16
17	18	19	20	21	22	23
24	25	26	27	28	29	30
31						

My shepherd, my Lord, my Savior, lead me beside the still waters. Lie with me in the green pastures. Restore my soul. Lead me down the paths of *Your* choosing today. With You by my side, I fear no evil. You are my comfort and my guide. I am happy in Your presence.

to-do list

SUNDAY, October 24

MONDAY, October 25

TUESDAY, October 26

WEDNESDAY, October 27

THURSDAY, October 28

FRIDAY, October 29

SATURDAY, October 30

to-do list

He makes me lie down in green pastures, he leads me beside quiet waters.
Psalm 23:2 niv

November 2027

SUNDAY	MONDAY	TUESDAY	WEDNESDAY
31	1	2 *Election Day*	3
7 *Daylight Saving Time Ends*	8	9	10
14	15	16	17
21	22	23	24
28	29	30	1

THURSDAY	FRIDAY	SATURDAY
4	5	6
11 *Veterans Day*	12	13
18	19	20
25 *Thanksgiving Day*	26	27
2	3	4

notes

October

S	M	T	W	T	F	S
					1	2
3	4	5	6	7	8	9
10	11	12	13	14	15	16
17	18	19	20	21	22	23
24	25	26	27	28	29	30
31						

December

S	M	T	W	T	F	S
			1	2	3	4
5	6	7	8	9	10	11
12	13	14	15	16	17	18
19	20	21	22	23	24	25
26	27	28	29	30	31	

Heavenly Father,
in all things,
I choose to
praise You.

Goals for the Month

The church of the living God is the strong foundation of truth.
1 Timothy 3:15 CEV

October–November 2027

S	M	T	W	T	F	S
	1	2	3	4	5	6
7	8	9	10	11	12	13
14	15	16	17	18	19	20
21	22	23	24	25	26	27
28	29	30				

God, sometimes life is so messy. Nothing has been going right. All I want to do is throw up my hands in frustration. But that is not of You, Lord. You are not a God of disorder but a God of peace. Help me, Lord, to be at peace now as I come to You in prayer. Help me to rest in Your presence and gain Your strength to meet the challenges of this day.

to-do list

SUNDAY, October 31 *Halloween*

MONDAY, November 1

TUESDAY, November 2 *Election Day*

WEDNESDAY, November 3

THURSDAY, November 4

FRIDAY, November 5

SATURDAY, November 6

to-do list

For God is not a God of disorder but of peace.
1 Corinthians 14:33 NIV

November 2027

S	M	T	W	T	F	S
	1	2	3	4	5	6
7	8	9	10	11	12	13
14	15	16	17	18	19	20
21	22	23	24	25	26	27
28	29	30				

Oh God, I long for Your presence and Your touch. Deliver me from worry, fear, and distress. Bind me with Your love and forgiveness as I rest in You. Fill me with Your power and Your strength to meet the challenges of this day. Thank You, Lord, for the way You are working in my life. Keep me close to You throughout this day.

to-do list

- [ ]
- [ ]
- [ ]
- [ ]
- [ ]
- [ ]
- [ ]
- [ ]
- [ ]
- [ ]
- [ ]
- [ ]
- [ ]
- [ ]
- [ ]

SUNDAY, November 7 *Daylight Saving Time Ends*

MONDAY, November 8

TUESDAY, November 9

WEDNESDAY, November 10

THURSDAY, November 11

Veterans Day

FRIDAY, November 12

SATURDAY, November 13

to-do list

- [ ]
- [ ]
- [ ]
- [ ]
- [ ]
- [ ]
- [ ]
- [ ]
- [ ]
- [ ]
- [ ]
- [ ]
- [ ]
- [ ]
- [ ]
- [ ]

*Lord, be gracious to us;
we have waited for You.
Be their strength every
morning, our salvation also
in the time of distress.*

Isaiah 33:2 NASB

November 2027

S	M	T	W	T	F	S
	1	2	3	4	5	6
7	8	9	10	11	12	13
14	15	16	17	18	19	20
21	22	23	24	25	26	27
28	29	30				

Lord, fill me with Your strength and direct my ways so I can successfully press through the temptation of sin. I want to remain obedient to Your leadership. I don't want to take Your mercy and grace for granted. Help me to focus on what is pure and holy in Your sight.

to-do list

- [ ]
- [ ]
- [ ]
- [ ]
- [ ]
- [ ]
- [ ]
- [ ]
- [ ]
- [ ]
- [ ]
- [ ]
- [ ]
- [ ]
- [ ]

SUNDAY, November 14

MONDAY, November 15

TUESDAY, November 16

WEDNESDAY, November 17

THURSDAY, November 18

FRIDAY, November 19

SATURDAY, November 20

to-do list

- [ ]
- [ ]
- [ ]
- [ ]
- [ ]
- [ ]
- [ ]
- [ ]
- [ ]
- [ ]
- [ ]
- [ ]
- [ ]
- [ ]
- [ ]
- [ ]

So I say, let the Holy Spirit guide your lives. Then you won't be doing what your sinful nature craves. . . . Since we are living by the Spirit, let us follow the Spirit's leading in every part of our lives.

GALATIANS 5:16, 25 NLT

November 2027

S	M	T	W	T	F	S
	1	2	3	4	5	6
7	8	9	10	11	12	13
14	15	16	17	18	19	20
21	22	23	24	25	26	27
28	29	30				

I try and try, but my efforts accomplish nothing when I have not come first to You in prayer. I need to do things in Your strength, for otherwise I am useless. I need Your power behind me when I speak. I need Your strength. Allow Your Word to speak to me. Guide my way by Your gentle voice. May my spirit and Yours become one this day.

to-do list

- [ ]
- [ ]
- [ ]
- [ ]
- [ ]
- [ ]
- [ ]
- [ ]
- [ ]
- [ ]
- [ ]
- [ ]
- [ ]
- [ ]
- [ ]

SUNDAY, November 21

MONDAY, November 22

TUESDAY, November 23

WEDNESDAY, November 24

THURSDAY, November 25 *Thanksgiving Day*

FRIDAY, November 26

SATURDAY, November 27

to-do list

[Jesus said,] "The Spirit alone gives eternal life. Human effort accomplishes nothing. And the very words I have spoken to you are spirit and life."

JOHN 6:63 NLT

December 2027

SUNDAY	MONDAY	TUESDAY	WEDNESDAY
28	29	30	1
5	6	7	8
12	13	14	15
19	20	21 *First Day of Winter*	22
26	27	28	29

THURSDAY	FRIDAY	SATURDAY
2	3	4
9	10	11
16	17	18
23	24 *Christmas Eve / Hanukkah Begins at Sundown*	25 *Christmas Day*
30	31 *New Year's Eve*	1

notes

November

S	M	T	W	T	F	S
	1	2	3	4	5	6
7	8	9	10	11	12	13
14	15	16	17	18	19	20
21	22	23	24	25	26	27
28	29	30				

January

S	M	T	W	T	F	S
						1
2	3	4	5	6	7	8
9	10	11	12	13	14	15
16	17	18	19	20	21	22
23	24	25	26	27	28	29
30	31					

Goals for the Month

Wait on the Lord;
be of good courage, and He
shall strengthen your heart;
wait, I say, on the Lord!
Psalm 27:14 NKJV

November–December 2027

S	M	T	W	T	F	S
			1	2	3	4
5	6	7	8	9	10	11
12	13	14	15	16	17	18
19	20	21	22	23	24	25
26	27	28	29	30	31	

Jesus, please be the Lord and Savior of my life. I confess my sins to You. Take my life and purge me from all that is ungodly and of this world. Fill me with new life. Make me a new creature, filled with Your Spirit. Without You I am nothing, but in You I can reach my full potential.

to-do list

- [ ]
- [ ]
- [ ]
- [ ]
- [ ]
- [ ]
- [ ]
- [ ]
- [ ]
- [ ]
- [ ]
- [ ]
- [ ]
- [ ]
- [ ]

SUNDAY, November 28

MONDAY, November 29

TUESDAY, November 30

WEDNESDAY, December 1

THURSDAY, December 2

FRIDAY, December 3

SATURDAY, December 4

to-do list

- [ ]
- [ ]
- [ ]
- [ ]
- [ ]
- [ ]
- [ ]
- [ ]
- [ ]
- [ ]
- [ ]
- [ ]
- [ ]
- [ ]
- [ ]
- [ ]

So whether you eat or drink, or whatever you do, do it all for the glory of God.

1 Corinthians 10:31 NLT

December 2027

S	M	T	W	T	F	S
			1	2	3	4
5	6	7	8	9	10	11
12	13	14	15	16	17	18
19	20	21	22	23	24	25
26	27	28	29	30	31	

Jesus, You knew that God's will was for You to give Your life so that others may experience God. You gave God total control and submitted to His will. Help me to do the same. I was created for a specific purpose. You have a plan for my life, and I want to complete everything You created me to accomplish. Help me to live my life according to Your ultimate plan.

to-do list

- [ ]
- [ ]
- [ ]
- [ ]
- [ ]
- [ ]
- [ ]
- [ ]
- [ ]
- [ ]
- [ ]
- [ ]
- [ ]
- [ ]
- [ ]

SUNDAY, December 5

MONDAY, December 6

TUESDAY, December 7

WEDNESDAY, December 8

THURSDAY, December 9

FRIDAY, December 10

SATURDAY, December 11

to-do list

We can make our plans, but the LORD *determines our steps.*
PROVERBS 16:9 NLT

December 2027

S	M	T	W	T	F	S
			1	2	3	4
5	6	7	8	9	10	11
12	13	14	15	16	17	18
19	20	21	22	23	24	25
26	27	28	29	30	31	

The Bible tells me that whatever I put my hand to will prosper. I am blessed in the city and in the field, when I come into my house and when I go out of it. Your blessing on my life provides for my every need. I ask for Your wisdom, Lord. Teach me to make the right choices and decisions for my life. You make me a blessing because I belong to You.

to-do list

- [ ]
- [ ]
- [ ]
- [ ]
- [ ]
- [ ]
- [ ]
- [ ]
- [ ]
- [ ]
- [ ]
- [ ]
- [ ]
- [ ]
- [ ]

SUNDAY, December 12

MONDAY, December 13

TUESDAY, December 14

WEDNESDAY, December 15

THURSDAY, December 16

FRIDAY, December 17

SATURDAY, December 18

to-do list

"I am the LORD *your God, who teaches you to benefit, who leads you in the way you should go."*
ISAIAH 48:17 NASB

December 2027

S	M	T	W	T	F	S
			1	2	3	4
5	6	7	8	9	10	11
12	13	14	15	16	17	18
19	20	21	22	23	24	25
26	27	28	29	30	31	

God, I know You are there. Even though I can't see You with my eyes, I sense Your presence when I pray. When I feel alone, I remember Your promise to never leave me. Thank You for always making Yourself known to me when I need You.

to-do list

- [ ] ....
- [ ] ....
- [ ] ....
- [ ] ....
- [ ] ....
- [ ] ....
- [ ] ....
- [ ] ....
- [ ] ....
- [ ] ....
- [ ] ....
- [ ] ....
- [ ] ....
- [ ] ....
- [ ] ....

SUNDAY, December 19

MONDAY, December 20

TUESDAY, December 21 *First Day of Winter*

WEDNESDAY, December 22

THURSDAY, December 23

FRIDAY, December 24

Christmas Eve / Hanukkah Begins at Sundown

SATURDAY, December 25

Christmas Day

to-do list

- [ ]
- [ ]
- [ ]
- [ ]
- [ ]
- [ ]
- [ ]
- [ ]
- [ ]
- [ ]
- [ ]
- [ ]
- [ ]
- [ ]
- [ ]
- [ ]

"The master said, 'Well done, my good and faithful servant. You have been faithful in handling this small amount, so now I will give you many more responsibilities. Let's celebrate together!'"

MATTHEW 25:23 NLT

December 2027–January 2028

S	M	T	W	T	F	S
			1	2	3	4
5	6	7	8	9	10	11
12	13	14	15	16	17	18
19	20	21	22	23	24	25
26	27	28	29	30	31	

Sometimes I look back at the things that didn't turn out quite right for me. I know I shouldn't focus on wrongs done to me or opportunities missed. You have set a great life before me, Lord, and I want to embrace it without the shadow of the past. Help me see the future with joy and expectation. My hope is in *You*!

to-do list

SUNDAY, December 26

MONDAY, December 27

TUESDAY, December 28

WEDNESDAY, December 29

THURSDAY, December 30

FRIDAY, December 31 *New Year's Eve*

SATURDAY, January 1 *New Year's Day*

to-do list

- [ ]
- [ ]
- [ ]
- [ ]
- [ ]
- [ ]
- [ ]
- [ ]
- [ ]
- [ ]
- [ ]
- [ ]
- [ ]
- [ ]
- [ ]
- [ ]

"When the Spirit of truth comes, he will guide you into all truth. He will not speak on his own but will tell you what he has heard. He will tell you about the future."

JOHN 16:13 NLT

Contacts

Name:

Address:

Phone: Cell:

Email:

Name:

Address:

Phone: Cell:

Email:

Name:

Address:

Phone: Cell:

Email:

Name:

Address:

Phone: Cell:

Email:

Name:

Address:

Phone: Cell:

Email:

Contacts

Name:

Address:

Phone: Cell:

Email:

Name:

Address:

Phone: Cell:

Email:

Name:

Address:

Phone: Cell:

Email:

Name:

Address:

Phone: Cell:

Email:

Name:

Address:

Phone: Cell:

Email:

Contacts

Name:

Address:

Phone: Cell:

Email:

Name:

Address:

Phone: Cell:

Email:

Name:

Address:

Phone: Cell:

Email:

Name:

Address:

Phone: Cell:

Email:

Name:

Address:

Phone: Cell:

Email:

Contacts

Name:

Address:

Phone: Cell:

Email:

Name:

Address:

Phone: Cell:

Email:

Name:

Address:

Phone: Cell:

Email:

Name:

Address:

Phone: Cell:

Email:

Name:

Address:

Phone: Cell:

Email:

Contacts

Name:

Address:

Phone: Cell:

Email:

Name:

Address:

Phone: Cell:

Email:

Name:

Address:

Phone: Cell:

Email:

Name:

Address:

Phone: Cell:

Email:

Name:

Address:

Phone: Cell:

Email:

Contacts

Name:

Address:

Phone: Cell:

Email:

Name:

Address:

Phone: Cell:

Email:

Name:

Address:

Phone: Cell:

Email:

Name:

Address:

Phone: Cell:

Email:

Name:

Address:

Phone: Cell:

Email:

Notes & Ideas

Notes & Ideas

Notes & Ideas

Notes & Ideas

Notes & Ideas

Notes & Ideas

Notes & Ideas

Notes & Ideas

Year at a Glance
CALENDARS

2028

JANUARY

S	M	T	W	T	F	S
						1
2	3	4	5	6	7	8
9	10	11	12	13	14	15
16	17	18	19	20	21	22
23	24	25	26	27	28	29
30	31					

FEBRUARY

S	M	T	W	T	F	S
		1	2	3	4	5
6	7	8	9	10	11	12
13	14	15	16	17	18	19
20	21	22	23	24	25	26
27	28	29				

MARCH

S	M	T	W	T	F	S
			1	2	3	4
5	6	7	8	9	10	11
12	13	14	15	16	17	18
19	20	21	22	23	24	25
26	27	28	29	30	31	

APRIL

S	M	T	W	T	F	S
						1
2	3	4	5	6	7	8
9	10	11	12	13	14	15
16	17	18	19	20	21	22
23	24	25	26	27	28	29
30						

MAY

S	M	T	W	T	F	S
	1	2	3	4	5	6
7	8	9	10	11	12	13
14	15	16	17	18	19	20
21	22	23	24	25	26	27
28	29	30	31			

JUNE

S	M	T	W	T	F	S
				1	2	3
4	5	6	7	8	9	10
11	12	13	14	15	16	17
18	19	20	21	22	23	24
25	26	27	28	29	30	

JULY

S	M	T	W	T	F	S
						1
2	3	4	5	6	7	8
9	10	11	12	13	14	15
16	17	18	19	20	21	22
23	24	25	26	27	28	29
30	31					

AUGUST

S	M	T	W	T	F	S
		1	2	3	4	5
6	7	8	9	10	11	12
13	14	15	16	17	18	19
20	21	22	23	24	25	26
27	28	29	30	31		

SEPTEMBER

S	M	T	W	T	F	S
					1	2
3	4	5	6	7	8	9
10	11	12	13	14	15	16
17	18	19	20	21	22	23
24	25	26	27	28	29	30

OCTOBER

S	M	T	W	T	F	S
1	2	3	4	5	6	7
8	9	10	11	12	13	14
15	16	17	18	19	20	21
22	23	24	25	26	27	28
29	30	31				

NOVEMBER

S	M	T	W	T	F	S
			1	2	3	4
5	6	7	8	9	10	11
12	13	14	15	16	17	18
19	20	21	22	23	24	25
26	27	28	29	30		

DECEMBER

S	M	T	W	T	F	S
					1	2
3	4	5	6	7	8	9
10	11	12	13	14	15	16
17	18	19	20	21	22	23
24	25	26	27	28	29	30
31						

2029

JANUARY

S	M	T	W	T	F	S
	1	2	3	4	5	6
7	8	9	10	11	12	13
14	15	16	17	18	19	20
21	22	23	24	25	26	27
28	29	30	31			

FEBRUARY

S	M	T	W	T	F	S
				1	2	3
4	5	6	7	8	9	10
11	12	13	14	15	16	17
18	19	20	21	22	23	24
25	26	27	28			

MARCH

S	M	T	W	T	F	S
				1	2	3
4	5	6	7	8	9	10
11	12	13	14	15	16	17
18	19	20	21	22	23	24
25	26	27	28	29	30	31

APRIL

S	M	T	W	T	F	S
1	2	3	4	5	6	7
8	9	10	11	12	13	14
15	16	17	18	19	20	21
22	23	24	25	26	27	28
29	30					

MAY

S	M	T	W	T	F	S
		1	2	3	4	5
6	7	8	9	10	11	12
13	14	15	16	17	18	19
20	21	22	23	24	25	26
27	28	29	30	31		

JUNE

S	M	T	W	T	F	S
					1	2
3	4	5	6	7	8	9
10	11	12	13	14	15	16
17	18	19	20	21	22	23
24	25	26	27	28	29	30

JULY

S	M	T	W	T	F	S
1	2	3	4	5	6	7
8	9	10	11	12	13	14
15	16	17	18	19	20	21
22	23	24	25	26	27	28
29	30	31				

AUGUST

S	M	T	W	T	F	S
			1	2	3	4
5	6	7	8	9	10	11
12	13	14	15	16	17	18
19	20	21	22	23	24	25
26	27	28	29	30	31	

SEPTEMBER

S	M	T	W	T	F	S
						1
2	3	4	5	6	7	8
9	10	11	12	13	14	15
16	17	18	19	20	21	22
23	24	25	26	27	28	29
30						

OCTOBER

S	M	T	W	T	F	S
	1	2	3	4	5	6
7	8	9	10	11	12	13
14	15	16	17	18	19	20
21	22	23	24	25	26	27
28	29	30	31			

NOVEMBER

S	M	T	W	T	F	S
				1	2	3
4	5	6	7	8	9	10
11	12	13	14	15	16	17
18	19	20	21	22	23	24
25	26	27	28	29	30	

DECEMBER

S	M	T	W	T	F	S
						1
2	3	4	5	6	7	8
9	10	11	12	13	14	15
16	17	18	19	20	21	22
23	24	25	26	27	28	29
30	31					